How to Hang a Spoon

Turnbull & Willoughby

HOW TO HANG A SPOON

Joe Martin

Second Printing April 1985

10 9 8 7 6 5 4

Manufactured in the United States of America

ISBN 0-943084-22-9

Photography by:
Ken Todd &
Art Wise Studios

Published by Turnbull & Willoughby Publishers, Inc.
1151 W. Webster, Chicago, IL 60614

About the author

Joe Martin is nuts. But he has been very, very successful at being nuts. His millions of fans read his two syndicated cartoons daily in almost 200 newspapers nationwide: **Willy 'n Ethel,** America's best loved loosers since the Honeymooners and **Porterfield,** the hottest of the new business cartoons.

He is also a screenwriter for ER — Emergency Room seen on CBS nad has written over 100 songs, none of which have been recorded.

His first book, **Warning: Willy 'N Ethel** was published in 1984 and is now in its third printing and his next book, **The Best of Willy 'N Ethel** is planned for late this year.

About the spoon

One of the most famous of all hanging spoons is the genuine Windsor model 150 mm stainless spoon. Its unique styling is based on its namesake, the Chrysler Windsor (circa 1947) and it carries all the streamlined good looks a top-notch hanging spoon requires.

What more suitable choice for the avid spoon hanger (and our cover) could there be? With its history and versatility, the Windsor remains the most sought after hanging spoon on the market today.

Author's note: For the perfect feel and weight, experienced spoonists often tape the handle of their spoon as they would a baseball bat or hockey stick. This added weight often helps the spoon (even the Windsor) adhere.

ACKNOWLEDGEMENTS

Thanks to everyone who allowed themselves to be photographed with spoons on their faces.

John Berg, Jr.
Karen Blake
Ute Brantsch
Ken Brautigam

Deborah Crocker
Tony Diviggiano
Todd Doney
Scott Doney

Gary Griffin
Lisa Gruber
Ted Hall
Deborah Klein

Tom Lanphear
Barbara Mandel
Richard Mann
Eve Madelaine O'Keefe-Mann

Jay Martin
Joe Martin
Marie Martin
Shelly Mulroy

Ward Mulroy
Willie J. Nelson
Tom Olcese
Karen Regnell

Deborah Schildgen
Greg Souers
Joseph Stevens
Allison Strobel

Mark Suchomel
Roberta Taub
Alan Toback

Sandra Toback
Anthony Vitale

and special thanks to nationally recognized attorney, Robert H. Friebert who, once again, was ahead of his time.

"The point I'm trying to make is that deep down inside every one of us is an absolutely fantastic ability to do one thing better than anyone else in the world. What if it's spoon hanging?"

1 WHAT'S THIS ALL ABOUT?

Spoon Hanging (spun hang ing) v. adv.
1. The art of, or inclination to, hang a spoon. 2. One who is of the persuasion to appendiginate ovid bowled, sprong-handled eating utensils on or about the face, its extremities or protruding parts (as in spoon hanging fool). 3. The act of appendiginating foreign objects spoonetically. 4. To make, form, affix, introduce or in some manner cause a spoon, ladle or convex metal plated scoop of any sort to adhere to the outer epidermic layer or skin tissue for no apparent reason.

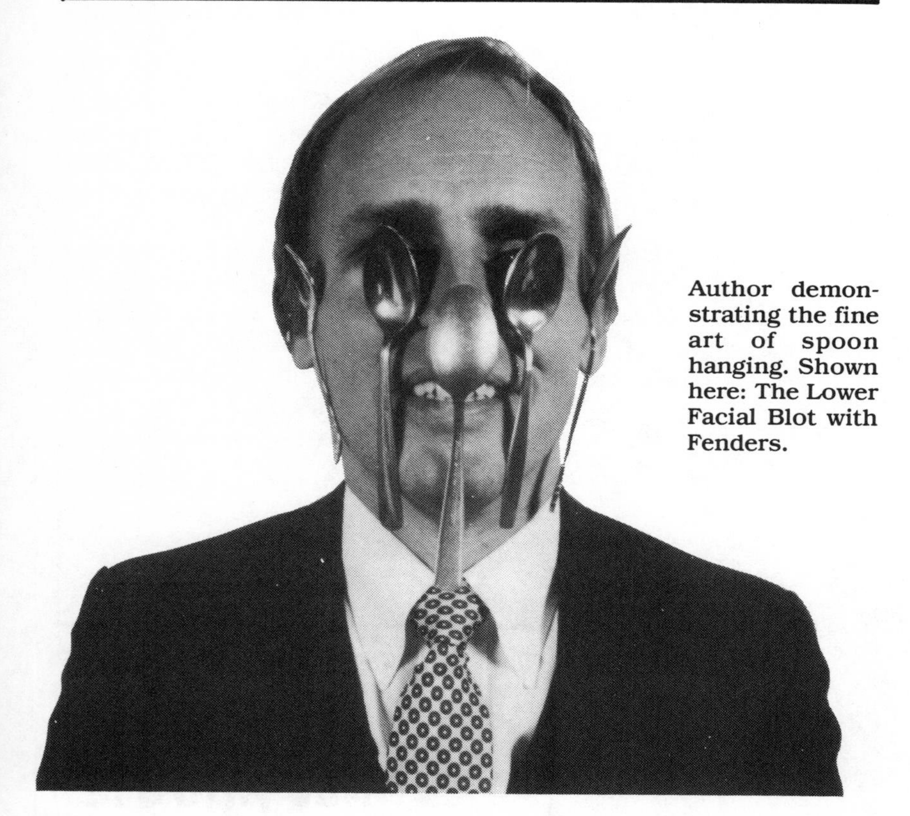

Author demonstrating the fine art of spoon hanging. Shown here: The Lower Facial Blot with Fenders.

Sure it all sounds easy. But in fact spoon hanging is much too complex to explain in simple dictionarial terms. So pay attention!

The following pages will deal with the how, when and where of spoon hanging. But more important they will also deal with the nagging question that has probably leaped first and foremost into your mind . . . that being WHY?

SPOON HANGING: WHY BOTHER?

Good question. First of all, let's face facts. The reason you have this book is because either you or someone that knows you well thinks that you should, or could, be capable of hanging spoons from your face. (What if you can't even do that? Not a pretty thought.) This book offers you the chance to find that one thing in life you can do better than anyone else.

Let me clarify this point (something I'm afraid I'm going to be doing a lot of if we're to make any headway.

Think of great sports names like Walter Payton, Jack Niclaus or Babe Ruth. Many people consider them national heroes. Yet without simple little games like golf, football or baseball where would they be?

I can answer that. They'd be right in back of you at the book store buying this book, that's where! The only difference between them and you is that they have found their holy grail and you haven't. They my careful reader, have found their niche in life . . . the one special thing they can do far better than anyone else. Think about it. What would Conners or MacEnroe be doing if tennis hadn't come along? They'd be driving cabs or selling things over the phone.

The jock who can't seem to make it to the top in a major sport might try his hand at spoon hanging.

The point I'm trying to make here is that deep inside every one of us is an absolutely fantastic ability to do ONE thing better than anyone else in the world. What if it's spoon hanging?

There are over 200 million people in this country who will never be best at anything. They will never reach the top ranks of football, baseball or hockey... not table tennis, not pool, not even shuffle board, darts, horseshoes, Scrabble or Trivial Pursuit. To all of these people I offer spoon hanging.

This could be it. The light at the end of the tunnel... the one thing you haven't tried ... the one thing that may give you what the MacEnroes and the Paytons of the world have. You could finally become the Best in the World at something and what glories and riches will await you.

Tony (Spoons) Lamott said it best when asked what spoon hanging had given him:

> "To the victor belongs the spoils and to the successful spoonist the world is their oyster. Money, fame and food are yours. And what woman can resist the charms of someone performing an 11 spoon Ultimate Facial Blot?"

This book will open your eyes to the art of Spoon Hanging and, in the process, its many benefits will be made clear. You will learn the joys of Aerobo-spoonercize, the Spoon Hanger's road to fitness; you will learn about your equipment, how to care for it and use it properly; you will be introduced to N.O.S.E. (National Organization of Spoonhanging Enthusiasts). Founded by the unforgettable Tony (Spoons) Lamott.

And, of course, you will learn how to hang spoons. From the incredibly basic one spoon monte to the 3 spoon lower facial blot and on to the more difficult 12-16 spoon combination hangs, a whole new world awaits you. This **could** be it! Your last chance at fame and fortune. Your last chance to be great at **something. DON'T SCREW IT UP!**

"Are you beginning to get that little tingly feeling running down your back? This could be the big time . . . the dream."

2 YOUR FIRST HANG

YOUR FIRST HANG

Remember your first kiss? Remember the first time you drove a car? Your first day on your very first job? Do you remember how nervous you were the day you took your first step; all wobbly, grabbing as tight as you could with those tiny fingers, praying that the coffee table wouldn't tip? Who could forget those moments? You wanted everything to be perfect, it was BIG-TIME important. Well, hanging your first spoon is no different and no matter how much detail I go into explaining just how this thing is supposed to be done, there's not a doubt in my mind that you'll find some way to botch it up.

Since this is your first hang pay careful attention. A major screw up here could leave deep psychological scars, not to mention physical ones. But be brave, persevere and keep repeating to yourself . . . any fool can do it!.

On the lecture circuit (I am constantly speaking on the social relevance of spoon hanging) I see people try and try again until they finally hang their first spoon. They keep trying because I'm there to show them it can really happen. For those of you who don't have the advantage of personal lessons, you'll just have to use the photos as your incentive. (The other trick is to learn all about Pant Fogulation but we'll get into that in a moment).

THE FIRST TIME

The Normal Method

Step #1 Grip a warm spoon by its handle . . . bend your head back slightly and rest the spoon on your nose as shown.

Step #2 Let go of handle. If there is any noise whatsoever at this point, pick up spoon and try again. This may take longer than I thought. Proceed.

Step #3 The spoon should now be resting on your nose with your head tilted back. Slowly slide the spoon foward. Don't let go of the handle until you feel it catch. This is a subtle thing, not an anchor taking hold so don't expect bells to go off.

Step #4 Tilt your head forward as you slowly and carefully let go of the spoon. If you're sweating and your fingers stick to the spoon, you have found a sure way to foul it up. Hopefully the spoon should begin to feel secure on your nose. Continue to tilt your head forward. Is it necessary for me to tell you to stop before you're bent over?

This is either the easiest part, or the hardest. Your head should be perfectly straight and the spoon should be pleasantly dangling from the end... If it's not, repeat the process. If it doesn't come right away just keep repeating to yourself, "Any Fool Can Do It" and pretty soon you'll have it.

THE MARTIN METHOD

The Spoonists the world over swear by the Normal Method, for fast and efficient results a viable alternative for you might be the spoonetically sound Martin Method.

The primary difference between these two methods is the use of the index finger as a conductor of heat to the nosal area of hanging. In the Normal Method the handle is gripped as the bowl is placed on the nose (proboscibalic tip). During the

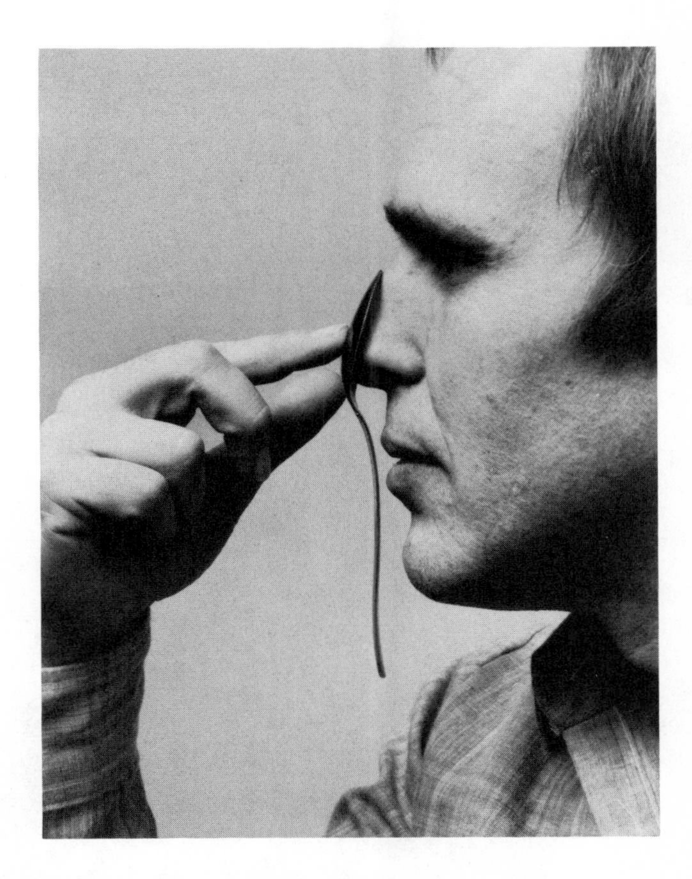

Fig. A. Author demonstrating his very own "Martin Method".

Martin Method, the outer Pissantic Grub is held to the nose (or anywhere on the face) and the cohesional process commences (see fig. 1). NOTE: Pant Fogulation, (as always,) is extremely important. Whichever method you select the spoon must be body temperature.

Step #1 Place the spoon against your face and press lightly with your index finger (see fig. A).

Fig. B. Press lightly with index fingers.

Fig. C. "I did it!"

Step #2 Focus both of your rotating orbs on a point at eye level. This should be a stationary point. **Concentrate on this point.** There are those who feel there is a metaphysical side to Spoon Hanging and, if that explains why this method works, I'm all for it. The fact is, if you follow these suggestions, the spoon will adhere and you can start to think about taking your finger away.

Step #3 With your head level and your concentration solidly welded on that stationary point you are now ready to find out if your efforts are to be rewarded. Slowly and carefully remove your finger from the spoon. If it drops, you've fouled up somewhere. Either you didn't read the directions properly, weren't paying attention as usual, or you're just not cut out for anything that requires the least bit of thought.

Step #4 If the spoon holds, try to attract someone's attention. Wave your arms if you have to but get someone to notice. Do this and you'll always have a point of reference for this great moment in your life . . . the day you hung your first spoon. (Make sure you do this **only** if the spoon is on your nose. Very few people will find it noteworthy that you **can't** get a spoon to hang).

Pant Fogulation

Pant Fogulation is the process that produces the magical bonding between spoon and nose. When you first pick up the spoon it will be cold and won't adhere to a room-temperature nose. Pant Fogulation gets the spoon in hanging form quickly.

Cup the spoon bowl in your hand and bring it up near your lips, which you have open in an "O" formation.

Envelop the spoon with your lips (IMPORTANT: DO NOT ALLOW THE SPOON TO TOUCH THE LIPS), and **pant** or breathe through your mouth to **fog** up the spoon with your hot breath.

Quickly move spoon to nose. Usually Pant Fogulation is repeated several times before each hang attempt. Eventually this sure-fire gimmick will become second nature to you, like breathng out and breathing in.

"Rule of thumb:
Cold spoons are for eating"
— Tony (Spoons) Lamott

THE VARSITY METHOD

Especially for those on Athletic Scholarships.

1. Pick up spoon using thumb and index finger (as shown). Most spoons have a slight arch where the handle meets the bowl, this is the best place to

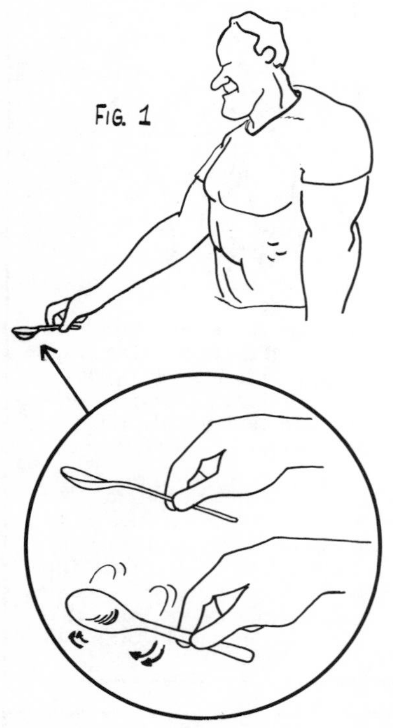

grip your spoon and was designed for just that purpose.

2. The Twist Pick Up (optional) The two illustrations show the two-step process most often used . . .

As the spoon is picked up, (fig. 1) apply slight pressure to the left side of the handle while pressing it firmly against the index finger. Note twisting motion (fig 2.) The spoon should now be sideways in preparation for Step 3, the elbow bend.

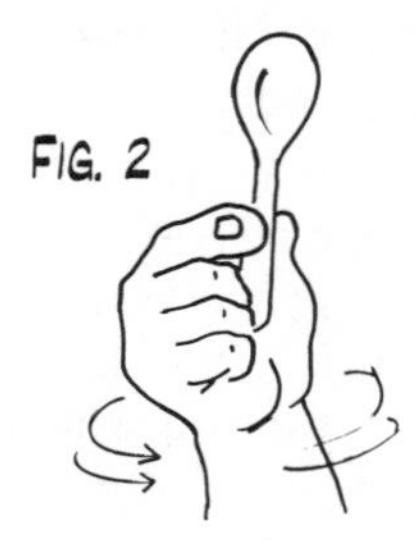

3. Holding the spoon firmly, begin to bend your elbow while at the same time twisting your wrist so that the bowl of the spoon is facing you (flatly). Carefully bend your elbow until the spoon reaches your nose, the more you bend the elbow the closer the spoon will come.

Take special care to stop the moment the spoon makes contact with your nasal tip. (Serious damage could result if this step is not followed with caution.)

Do Not Bend The Elbow Too Far.

Step 3 should not be attempted alone until the spoonist is thoroughly familiar with the process.

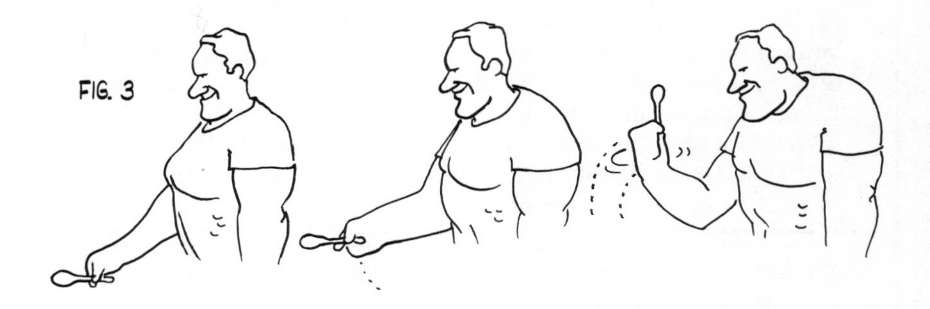

Best results are achieved by executing the bend and twist as slowly as possible at first, with accuracy the main goal. Then gradually as your skill increases you may also increase the speed.

Some Things You Should Know (Part I)

It may appear to you from time to time that I'm pulling a lot of this out of thin air. I believe the technical term is "making it out of whole cloth", and in a lot of cases, I don't deny it. Sometimes it's best not to get bogged down with details. Pushing ahead is the key. However, there is a point to be made about the technical, (true) side of Spoon Hanging.

It was my hope that the clever reader would find a solid undercurrent of actual truth to all of this. But for those of you who need a building to fall on them I think it might be wise to go over a few points.

(1) Never forget: The spoon must be warm! Body temperature seems to be perfect. Practice Pant Fogulation

(2) HeadTilt: If you find it difficult to hang the spoon on your nose, the problem may be eliminated by a simple adjustment in the tilt of your head. It should not be too far back nor should it be too far forward. Experiment. For most hangers it's the spoonetically erect stance (military drill) with a slight **forward** tilt that seems to do the trick. (a slight lowering of the chin)

(3) Warm Up Time: The more you work with your spoon the quicker and easier it is to hang. For competitions (especially the One-on-One) I recommend at least a five to ten minute warm-up time. Concentrate your practice on the area you'll be using (nose, forehead, cheek, etc.)

(4) The Drop-Slide Technique: To execute the basic one spoon monty (single spoon on the nose) another approach some find helpful is the drop slide. This is achieved through the simple maneuver of placing the spoon as high up on the nose as possible (the tipiscular point of the nose at this state is at the base of the grub (spoonal bowl) and very near the handolic arch.

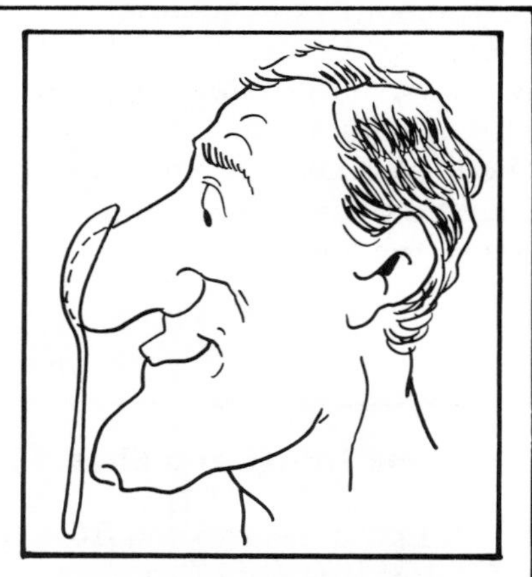

The spoon is held to the nose by applying pressure to the outer grubular (convex) area of the spoon with the index finger until the fusion process begins. NOTE: If this is done right the spoon will slowly slide down the frontal bone of the nose and come to rest on the nasal tip (probiscaball) where it should remain firmly for all the world to see.

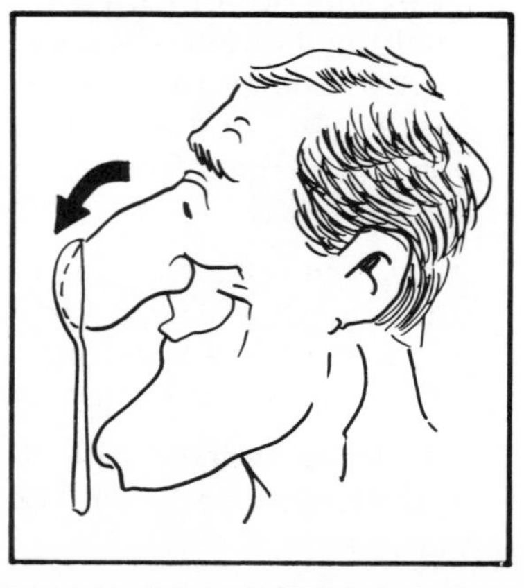

(5) Breathing: In the nosal hangs effective spoonal adhesion can be achieved through the use of the various B.C. (breath control) techniques. The B.C. techniques are merely extensions of the pant fogulation concept in that they allow the spoonist to keep the spoon as warm as possible. The most popular B.C. technique is the L.L.E. (lower lip extension) which is achieved by the simple process of extending the lower lip and then breathing upwards. You will notice that the air, diverted by the lip, will enter the convex bowloid area of the spoon known as the inner bowlictic or grub space. Retained here by the rim tiffs (see diagram chapter 4) a constant layer of heat is implanted.

(6) The Right Spoon: Choosing the right spoon is as important as choosing the right mate. If it doesn't fit or feel right you can always change. The point though is one can save himself some time if he experiments first. Test the spoons on the market.

Just because my publisher attached the famous Windsor model to this book, don't assume it's the best spoon for your face.

(7) Have Confidence: Don't be influenced by clear thinking logical people who try to turn you away from spoon hanging. There will always be those who lack the courage to make fools of themselves, pay them no mind . . . they are retarded and need the shelter of small grafitti coated minds like their own. Spoon Hangers must develop a thick skin. The man who can take a final exam or stand up in traffic court with a spoon on his nose is the same man who will show up at his own wedding or divorce with that same spoon tightly and defiantly stuck to his nose. It doesn't take a great deal of imagination to see that this fellow is going to be taking more flack than the next guy. So what! Right . . . who cares? That's the spirit! . . . we think.

Some Things You Should Know (Part II)

If you have trouble executing the one-spoon monty you should be tremendously discouraged. Performing the one-spoon monty for an experienced Spoon Hanger would be comparable to showing up at the park for a ball player.

If after one hour of serious effort you are still unable to hang the spoon on your nose, give it up, it's over. Chalk it up to experience. Get a nice chair, set it by your front window and watch the traffic go by, and look for my upcoming book, "Frustration . . . A Way of Life".

However, if you succeed in this basic hang the door to a whole new future is now open and waiting. This could be it. Are you beginning to get that little tingly feeling down your back? This could be the big time — the dream. Perhaps you've taken that first step towards immortality. This could be that one thing, the one great thing that nobody can do better than you. Then again, maybe it's not.

Can anyone hang a spoon?

"Don't look back, the worst is over. If you can hang one you can hang twenty."

3 MULTI-SPOON HANGS

AFTER THE MONTE

With the mastery of the incredibly simple one-spoon monty we've established one thing . . . we know you're not a klutz, which could have been and, in many cases, is a major stumbling block. Don't look back, the worst is over. If you can hang one you can hang twenty. All it takes is luck; forget determination, iron wills, positive thinking. Forget anything that sounds hard. If you're going to be a champion at this it's gonna be like falling off a log. The idea here is that this is **your thing.** If it's meant to be, it'll be easy. Don't worry about it. You're either gonna make it and be a hero, or you won't and you'll be back at McDonald's. Relax.

Coming up next is a series of more involved hangs that you should be able to waltz through with little or no effort. It may take a few tries but once you get the knack you'll have it. Remember we're still a long way from any tough stuff.

3-Spoon Hangs

Here are four variations on the classic 3-spoon hang

The Sphinx

Hyper-Spaz

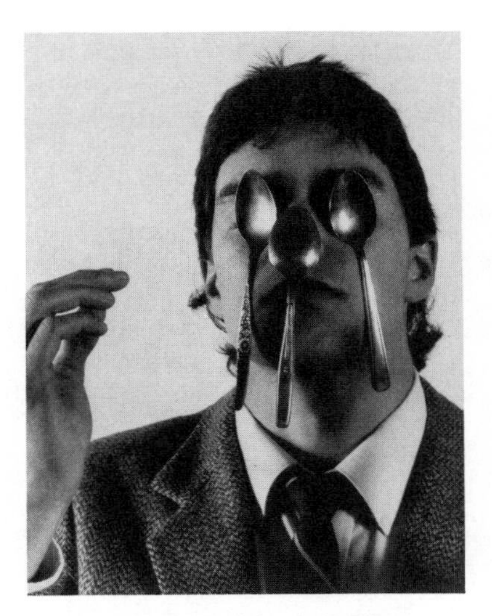

The Lower Facial Blot

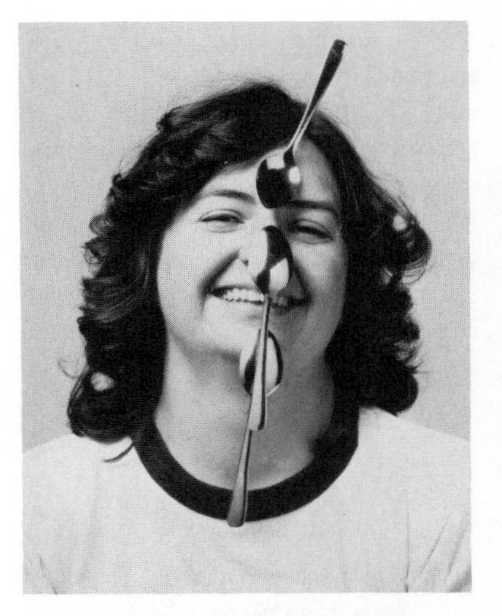

The Laditudinal Tri-bar

THE LOWER FACIAL BLOT

These are, of course, only a few examples of the many variations of 3-spoon hangs. The most popular and the easiest.

Following is a step-by-step guide to performing **The Lower Facial Blot,** possibly the easiest of the 3 spoon hangs. Because this is such an easy hang, performers often "dress-up their act" by doing imitations during the hang. This qualifies as an "expression" hang and of course, entitles the performer to extra degree of difficulty points. (Discussed in greater detail in chapter 8).

This is a great hang. If you master it you'll never have any trouble getting waiting on in a restaurant. There's just something about a face full of spoons . . . it seems to command attention.

Step #1

Start with the basic one spoon hang. If you are in a public place don't pay any attention to

the looks people are giving you; it can only bring disaster. Once you realize that these odd glances and disapproving stares are based on good solid reason, the game is up . . . you will have lost your nerve. Just wait until they see what's coming.

Step #2
Have your spoons ready . . . and be courageous. If you attempt this in a fine restaurant you'll find the staff to be very encouraging . . . the thought being the less noise you make the better. Naturally, the more successful you are the less spoons you will drop so there's a lot of team spirit as you're all working toward the same goal.

Step #3
This young lady is in the precise moment of completing the Lower Facial Blot. What you don't see are the eyes of the spectators staring in awe of this feat of bravado (and won't see it no matter where you

perform this feat). Mostly you'll see people rotating their index fingers around their ears and you may get a few old ladies tugging at their husband's sleeves . . . but not until you can hang five or six will you turn any heads.

Step #4
This young lady, having completed the basic Blot, is now going for degree of difficulty points. These are gained by incorporating other features into the hang: In this case our talented spoon hanger is doing impressions.

The Shelly Berman hang

FENDERS . . . THAT EXTRA SOMETHING

For that "extra something", Fenders are an interesting addition to any hang especially for those of you baby boomers who still remember the flat top.

What are the three most important things to consider when hanging a spoon? Location, location, location and the spoonist who wants to expand his horizons need look no farther than the sides of his head.

If you check the outer spoonal perimeter of your facial area of competition you'll find that just in front of your ear and just above the back of your cheek bone, there is a natural and structurally sound grippet just waiting to support your Fender spoon. Feel it with your fingers. Rotate them around. This will be similar to the motion you make during acute migraine headaches. If you are having trouble finding this area ask someone with small children. they will locate it for you immediately.

How to execute the Fender Hang.

Fig. #1
Now that you've found the place, it's time to get your spoons in position. Using your own ingenuity, arrange them so the bowloid (convex) area of the spoon is snugly implanted on the grippular area described above.

Place your fingers inside the bowls of the spoons and hold until you feel the cohesional process begin.

Fig. 1

Step #2

Have patience. This is not the easiest maneuver to get the hang of and complete spoonal adherence may take a few moments. Use this time wisely. It's an ideal opportunity to practice your expression hangs (Note Fig. #2. This young lady is showing a flawless execution of the always popular "twister tongue bite" shown here with a "leftular veer").

Use the chart on the following page as a handy reference when attempting any of the 842 multi-spoon hangs currently recognized by N.O.S.E. (i.e. 1+2+3= The Sphinx. A Sphinx 6&7=A Sphinx with Fenders. A Lower Facial Blot is composed of 1+4+5.)

Spoonists have learned it is often easier to refer to complicated hangs by listing their component hangs rather than individual spoonal placement. Therefore, a Global Strobel would be described as a Quadraspoon with Full Fenders, 2 Jowels a Double Richard and a Drool, rather than spoons 6, 7, 8, 9, 10, 11, 12, 13, 22, 23, 24, 25 and 27. Whew!!

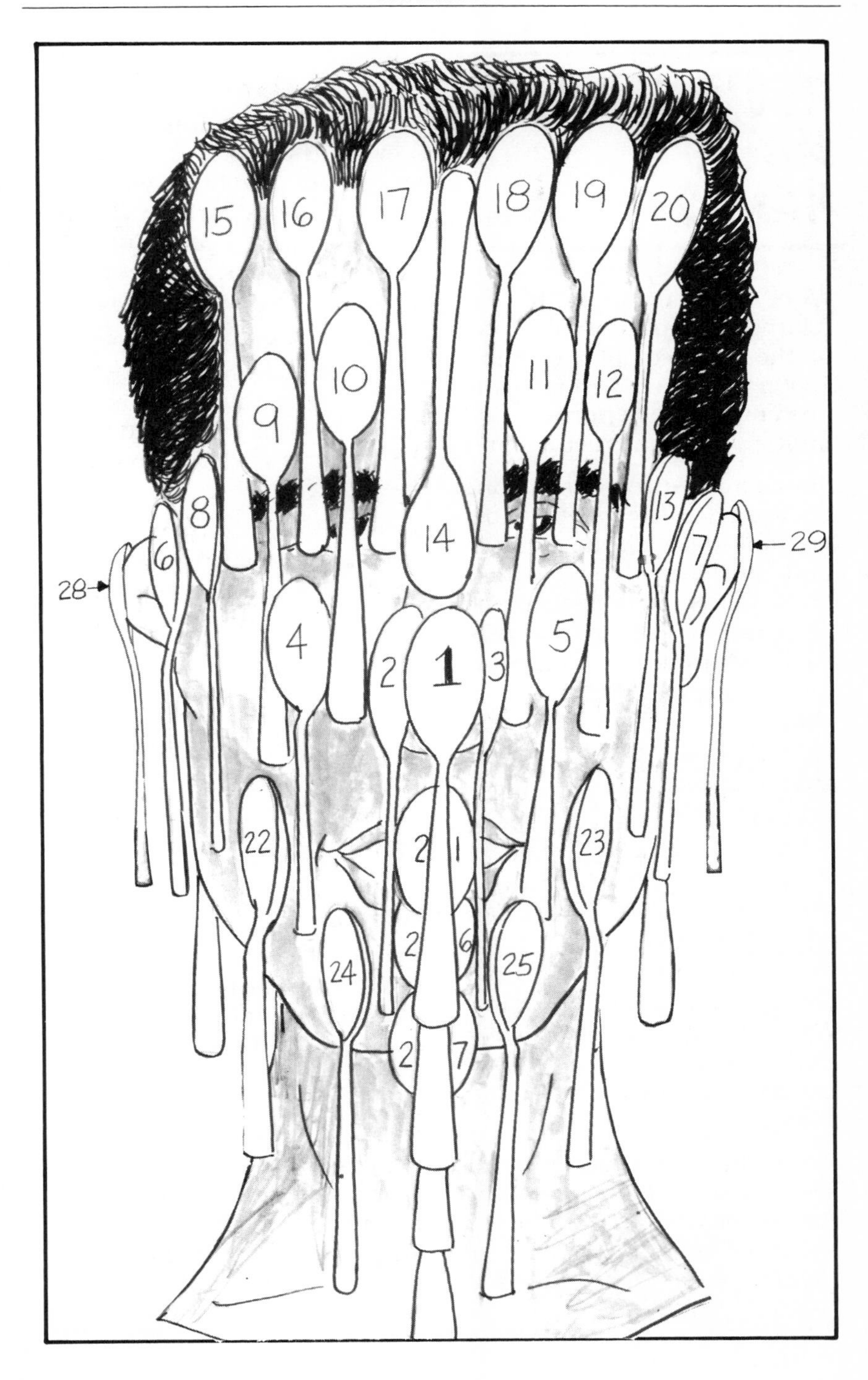
15
16
17
18
19
20
9
10
11
12
8
13
6
7
14
28
29
4
2
1
3
5
22
21
23
26
24
25
27

REVIEW: MULTI-HANGS

Whether you're attempting the relatively simple Orb Shadows or the more complex Quadra-spoon with Full Fenders, the procedure for performing all multi-spoon hangs is the same:

First make sure your spoons are warm (review the Pant Fogulation Method). It is often difficult to keep 5 or 6 spoons warm and ready without some preparation (spoon hangers should have some degree of resourcefulness. Figure out a way).

Place as many spoons on the facial zone of competition as possible at one time. If you put the spoons on one at a time, by the time you get to the last one the first one may have fallen off, and pretty soon you'll begin to take on the look of an old Laurel and Hardy routine. Watch for this, it's called the Dominodial Spoonal Effect and at times can be extremely frustrating.

Remember, in competition you are only required to maintain the spoonal formation for a count of ten (a slurred but legible "ten" is the formal N.O.S.E. standard.)

Also, if you are having difficulty, keep the Martin Method in mind. Keep a finger on the bowl of the spoon at the point of contact. The heat generated by your body will be transmitted through your finger to the spoon and cause it to cohese to the Skinial layer.

I recommend an assistant for any serious competition where wagering is involved. Keeping lots of spoons warm and within reach is easier if you have help.

Don't expect miracles. Just keep practicing and before you know it you'll be competing and winning tournaments regularly. Some day you might even find yourself on the receiving end of a coveted N.O.S.E. Around the World award.

Stranger things have happened.

Additional Multi-Spoon Hangs.

On the previous pages I have shown you only a few of the basic multi-spoon hangs. These are the most popular of the 841 hangs currently recognized by N.O.S.E. Following are the 24 definitive N.O.S.E. hangs that every spoon hanger must know. Study them closely. You will meet them in all N.O.S.E. sanctioned competitions. Practice them. Be ready.

THE TWENTY-FOUR

Although N.O.S.E. currently recognizes 851 separate hangs (842 of which are multi-spoon hangs), THE TWENTY-FOUR are the most exciting and innovative of all the hangs. Over the years each of THE TWENTY-FOUR has found a special place in the hearts of spoonists worldwide. As a result, many of the N.O.S.E. sanctioned competitions are based on these hangs.

The Around the World Meet

The Around the World Meet is the most common and the most interesting of all spoon hanging meets. It requires the participant to execute any 20 of THE TWENTY-FOUR.

The winner is the individual who completes the required number of hangs in the shortest time. In the case of ties the winner is determined through Degree of Difficulty Points.

The Regular Meet

The Regular Meet, for intermediate spoon hangers, only requires participants to select any 10 of THE TWENTY-FOUR.

The Quickie Meet

The Quickie Meet is great for the spoonist who desires the fun of competition, the thrills and the excitement but lacks the time. This competition allows participants to select only 6 of THE TWENTY-FOUR. (As usual, Expression Points, as well as Degree of Difficulty Points and diversionary tactics play a big part in deciding the winner).

"Not knowing the basic 24 hangs is as dangerous as being locked in a rubber room without a helmet."

Tony (Spoons) Lamott

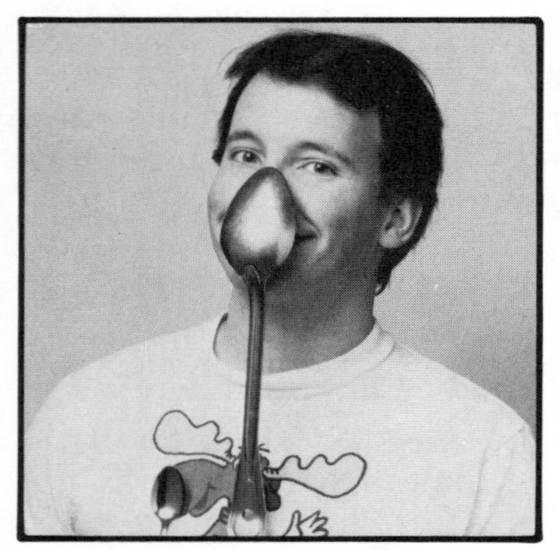

Lapaloza Ladle

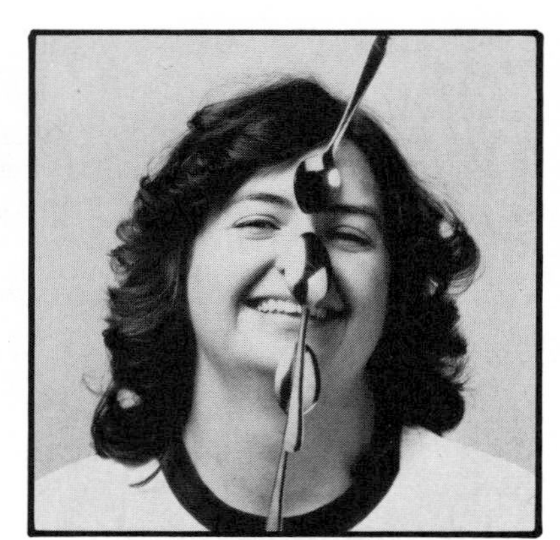

Laditudinal Tri-bar

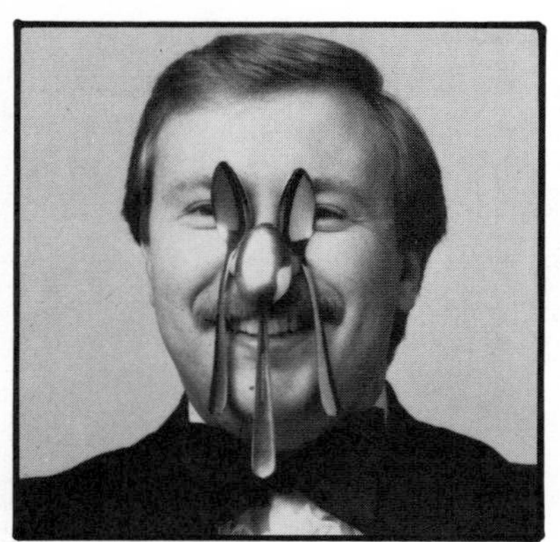

The Sphinx

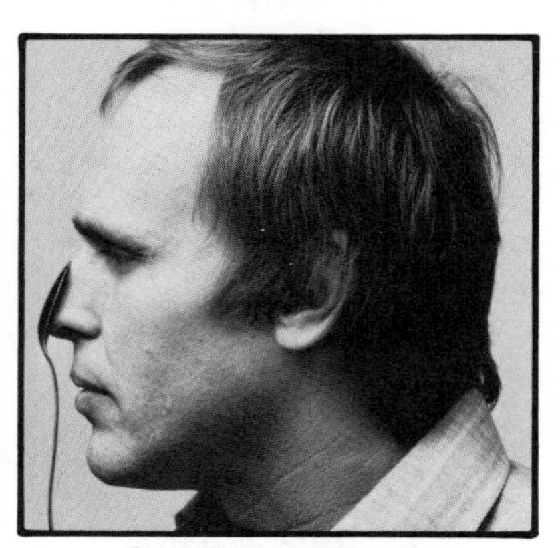

One Spoon Monte

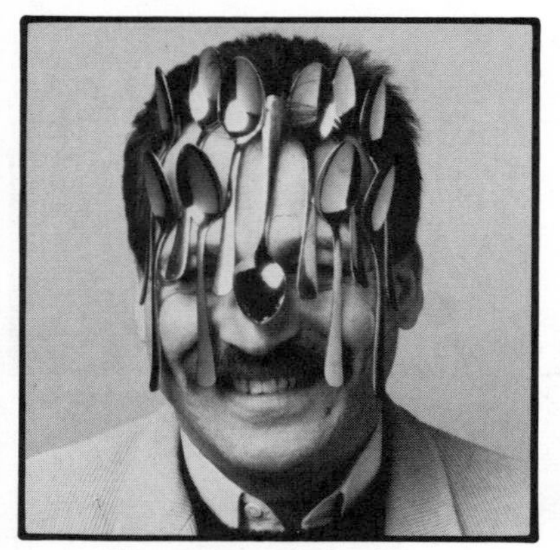

Upper Facial Blot

Chrome Dome

Gothic Spoons

Mother with Child & Spoon

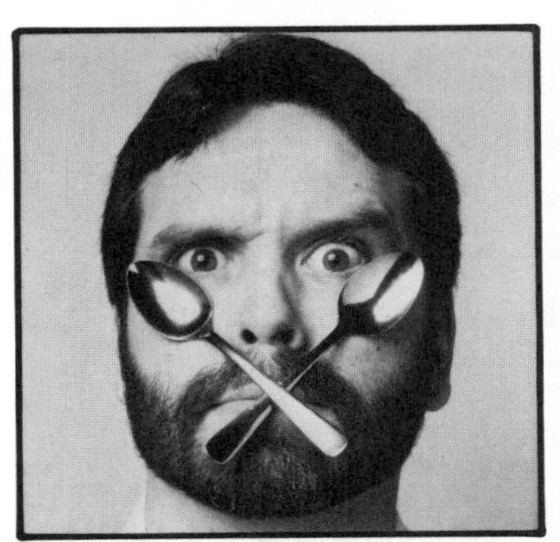

Jolly Roger

The Drool

Fenders

Crown with Chrome Dome

Hyper Spaz

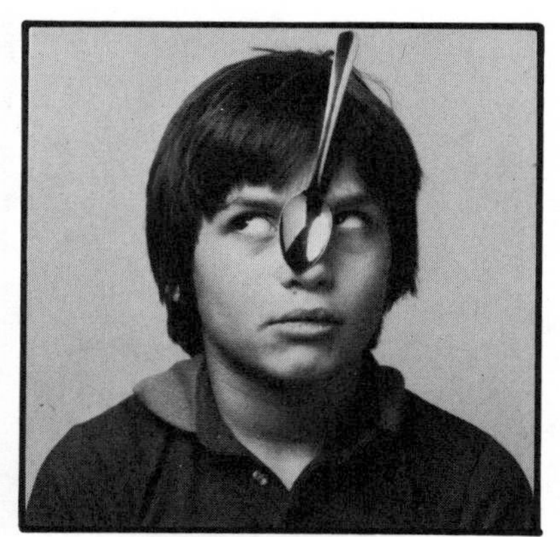

Multiple Mervis

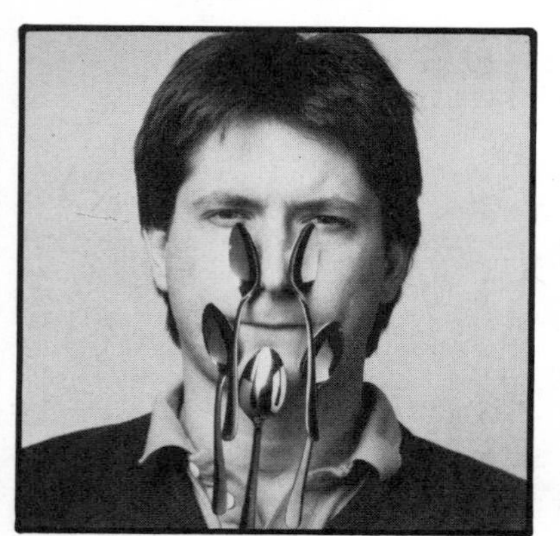

Fu Manchu

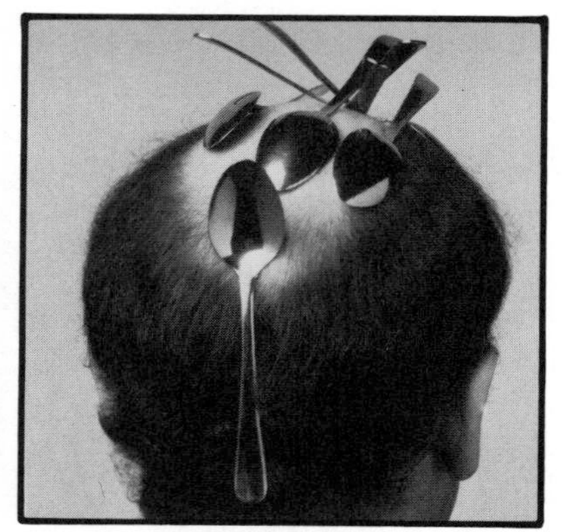

Bashful Blot

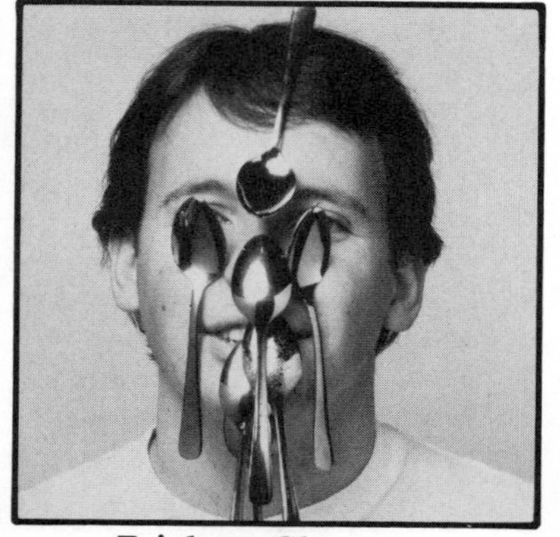

Friebert Cluster

Lip Dweller

The Cliff Hang

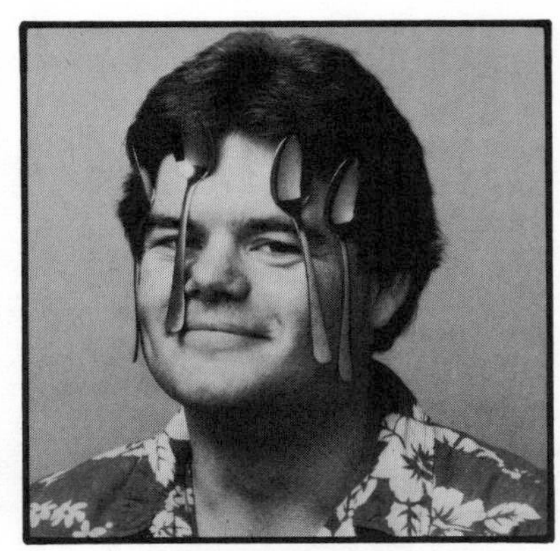

Quadra Spoons

Deluxe Lower Facial Blot

Vadarian Flying Horns

Double Richard

Ear Muffs

VERY UNOFFICIAL HANGS

"The football player must go to the stadium, card player to the table, the tennis player to the court but for the spoon hanger, the face is the place."

4 YOUR EQUIPMENT

YOUR EQUIPMENT

Skiers talk of un-touched snow and the exhilaration they experience gliding through it. Great runners tell of their euphoric highs. Champions of golf, baseball and football are never at a loss to describe the peaks of excitement they have reached.

For spoon hangers, that brief wonderful moment when the spoon hanger and the spoon become one . . . that single solitary unique moment is called THE FIT and it is this which all hangers strive for.

Achieving the perfect fit requires the spoon hanger to "know his equipment," so take your time and carefully familiarize yourself with the two basic pieces of spoon hanging equipment: the face and the spoon.

THE FACE

In spoon hanging **you** are the most important piece of equipment, or more specifically, your face is. Get to know it spoonetically.

Those indentations and deep fissures that cause people to turn and laugh, those gaping nooks and crannies that create ripples of low whispers whenever you enter a room may be the proud new hanging grounds of spoons of all shapes and sizes. A whole world of opportunity awaits those features once reserved only for ridicule. All you need is your imagination and your belief.

Study your face in the way a mountain climber might study a peak. Sir Edmund Hillary didn't just happen to be walking by Mount Everest one day and all of a sudden turn to his pals with a "last one to the top is a rotten egg." Of course not, these things take planning. Maps are made; charts and graphs are studied.

Take a close look at your features. Where would a spoon look good? Where would it look bad? Does your forehead hang like a cliff over two pig-like orbs rotating wildly? Can you see the tip of your chin? If so, you're a very lucky person and, as far as spoon hanging is concerned, you will be very successful.

But not everyone is blessed with such spoonetically useful features. Most of you will have to spend countless hours face-searching, and experimenting with all types of spoons to find the "FIT."

The following pages contain illustrations depicting various facial characteristics prevalent in most spoon hanging crowds. Keep in mind we are only highlighting a small segment of the usual facial grippetts[1]. A short walk down any crowded street will tell you that the combinations of noses, chins, cheeks, brows and other facial paraphernalia are as limitless as the flavors of ice cream.

If you find yourself or your friends among the following illustrations, follow the helpful tips included; they will speed you along the road to successful spoon hanging.

Not Everyone is Blessed with Spoonetically Useful Features

Your Equipment

The Noses

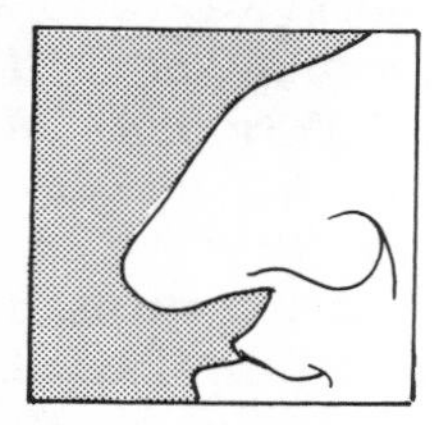

The Hook (or Bevel Beak). Usually accompanied by a fine set of tunnulationally sound expandoports, this is fine spooning ground for the Triple and certainly the one to beat in any fast draw.

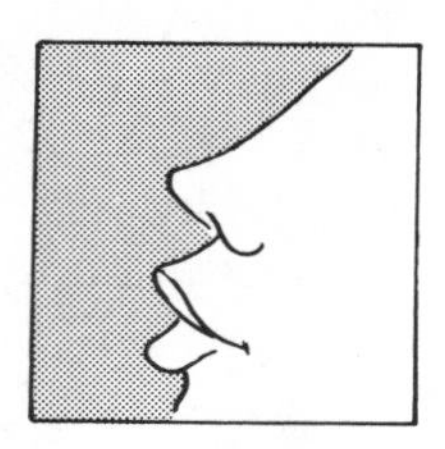

The Button Nose (or Probiscofied Dot). Although its size precludes any chance at the Triple, it is great for one-on-one competition because of a compact style that makes it great for travel.

The Foreheads

The Frontular Flat Head. This glacier-like effect can be frustrating to even the most dedicated spoon hanger but it is still much preferred to the cosmetically surprising Topular Flat Head.

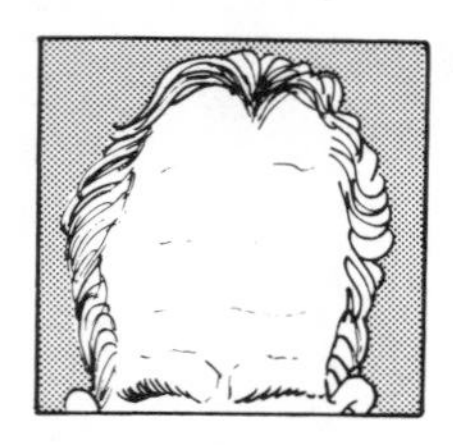

The Rim Cliff (Orb Shades). This wonderful awning-like effect offers the spoon hanger the ideal home for the Quadra-Spoon. It's also a great foundation for the building of the Upper Facial Blot.

The Chins

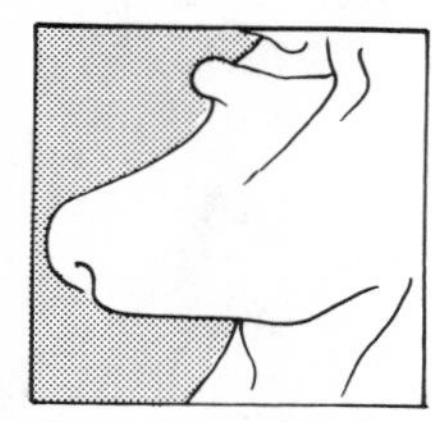

The Fearless (or Cleftulated Hammer Chin). Also known as the Fosdick. Throughout history from Greek mythology to Dudley Do Right, this chin has shown durability and lasting style.

The Reverse Chin. Also known as the Weasel or Yellowback, this contour has an inward slope that makes it less than desirable for most hangs.

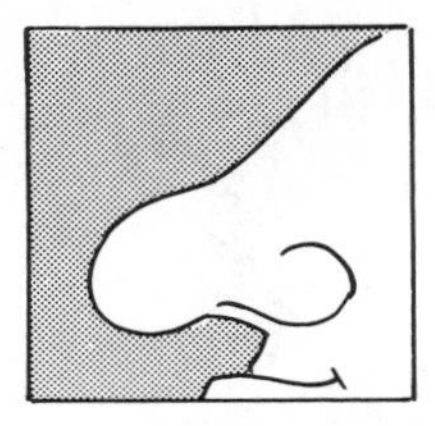

The Edison (or Bulb Nose). With its clearly delineated probiscaballic tip, it ranks at the top of all competitive noses.

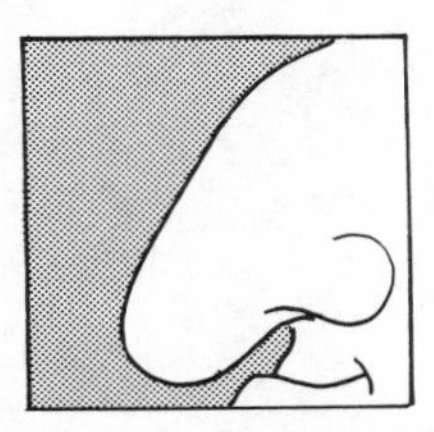

The Romanesque. This aquiline contour offers the ideal slope for the Drop-slide Technique. As all spoon hangers know, no formidable opponent can be found than those possessing "Caeser's Beezers."

The Folliculated Dome. Not as spacious as the Chrome Dome, this is the ideal site for the Upper Facial Blot, especially when one takes advantage of the harbors or coves of the widow's peak.

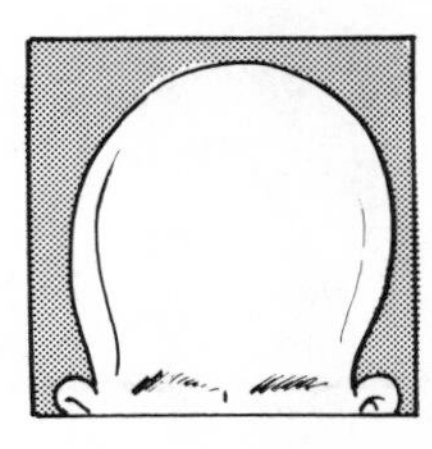

The Chrome Dome (or Henry). Offers maximum spoonal area for competition and makes execution of the awesome Double Upper Facial Blot a reality.

The Bowl (or Bucket Chin). This traditional model, with its workmanlike and highly functional qualities, need no longer remain limited to holding soup. It adapts well to all chinial hangs.

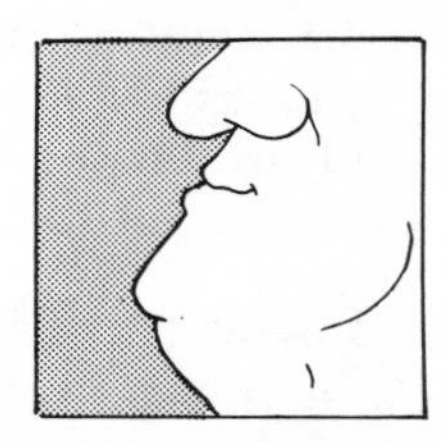

Twin Chins (or Orson's Wells). This healthy display of chinial property opens the door to the rotund hangs where jowls provide the imaginative spoon hanger with all the space he needs.

THE SPOON

The second most important piece of equipment is the specific spoon (or spoons) you choose to hang.

Spoons: A Brief History

The spoon is the oldest known eating tool developed by man. It was created just a little over 2 million years ago by the nomadic tribe of Neanderthals known as the Cromagtites (the ones that live down by the river*). Its earliest use was for cold soups (vichyssoise). The closest anthropological data can put the exact time of its creation at "around five o'clock." This was the time the Cromagtites and their families usually ate their largest meal of the day — the only one with a soup course.

*Approximate translation of the Fentonic dialect. Could also mean "the ones that live up from the river." (for further information and detailed anthropological data on these interesting people look for my book "The Ones That Live Somewhere Around the River")

It is important to note that the Cromagtite spoon which was made of stone could not be hung effectively. Only METAL spoons may be successfully used for this purpose.

The Modern Day Basic Spoon (itself)

The spoon's actual configuration (potswell or bowloid) is much the same now as it was 2 million years ago when it was first developed. The spoon shown here (fig. A) has the same formic handle and fingovial palmet adhesions the first Cromagtite spoon had. It also has the same convex (convexial with tin base) rim tiffs and the same arch grip which has made it so manageable and easy to pick up all these years. There has really been little change in the spoon's original concept.

NOTE: It is important that the spoon hanger be very familiar with the spoon chosen for hanging, its intricate design, structure and never changing parts. In the microcosmic world of precision spoon hanging, a thousandth of a speck of difference on a rim tiff may mean the loss of a crown.

Study the accompanying diagram with great care paying special attention to the individual parts of the spoon which give it the hangability for which it is known.

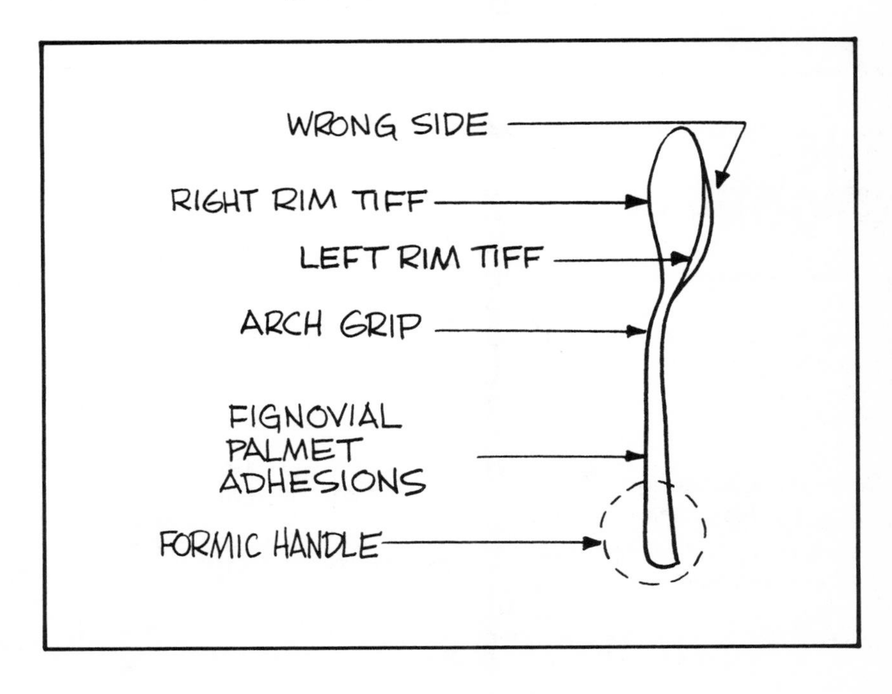

The Metalized Spoon

With the metalization of the spoon a whole new world opened up for the spoon hanger. For 2 million years spoon hangers were laughed at and ridiculed and for good reason — because of their foolish belief that they could hang a spoon from their face. This ridicule from their peers was well-founded, for in fact it is impossible to hang anything but a metal-based spoon.

Early Cromagtite Spoon (circa 2,000,000 B.C.)

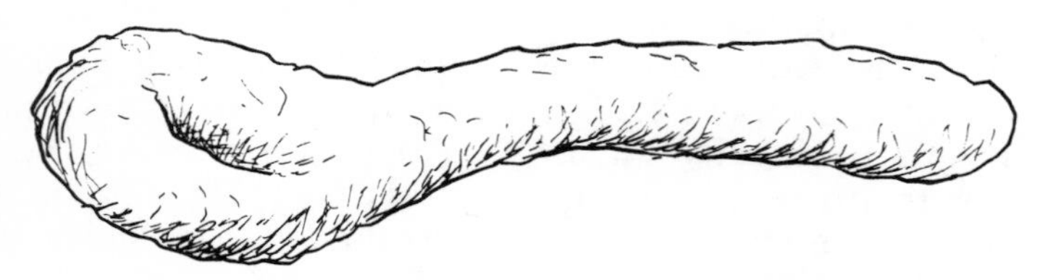

The latter developed stone (durable) spoon

Metalized spoon (hangable) circa 842 A.D.

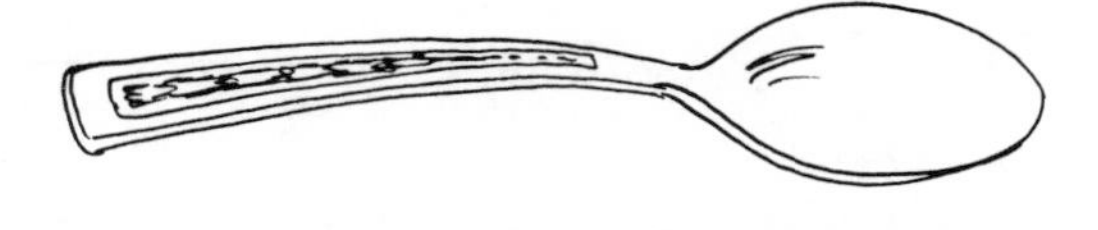

Cromagtite party pack

What Makes It Do That?

For many years the poor spoon hangers were under the impression that simply because the spoon was structured in the potswell or bowloid configuration it could be hung from the nose or face. We know now this is foolish, but imagine how funny it must have been when they first realized that for two million years they had all been wasting their time.

Fortunately the joy at the discovery that the new metalized spoon could now be hung far outweighed their bewilderment over the wasted years and they pushed ahead. The sport grew like wild fire. Handfuls of spoon hangers everywhere were all anxious to hang metal.

Here's How it Works

the best technical definition I can get on the subject comes from Dr. Helmet Veeters, the head of astro-physical research at our nation's largest nuclear facility who claims it's "a little like magic."

After waiting two million years who really cares why it hangs? The important thing is, what are we going to do about it, and how we can use this great gift. Shown here is a typical avid spoon hanger demonstrating the one-spoon monty with his new metalized spoon, (fig. B). Note how the nasal tip rests supportively in the hollow bowl shaped area of the spoon which we now call the "PISSANT."

For years this area was known only by the original name given it by the early Cromagtites, which was "the grub" or "place where the soup goes." With the advent of the metalized spoon and spoon hanging many new uses were found for this all too important part of the spoon, making the Cromagtite appellation all but obsolete.

With the introduction of metal the outer bowl which the Cromagtites called the "wrong side" now becomes the reversulated outer pissantic grub curve and the outer pissantic grubular grippet, two very key factors in spoon hanging. By placing your index finger at either of these points the heat generated will help to form a fissionatic bond between the spoon and your nose, a must in spoon hanging. (See Martin Method, Chapter Two).

A thorough understanding of the dangloidinal province is mandatory! The dangloidinal province is the area between the spoon's formic handle and your chin. The formic handle should at no time touch the chinial area. To do so would leave the spoon vulnerable to facial jostulation and probably droppage, the worst thing that can happen. Think about it, if the spoon is touching your chin and you start to talk, (extra points can be achieved by speech or facial contortions) you'll move the spoon, and doing that can dislodge it from the nose .

Note: In all spoon hangs only the pissant or the outer pissantic grub curve (and/or grippet) should be in contact with skinnial tissue. (There are some rare exceptions in the exotic hang category.)

I thought it important that the reader have a visual idea about what goes on biologically behind the spoon so I asked several medical experts, all highly respected in their fields, to submit the illustration they felt might best suit my purposes.

I chose this one . . .

---

[1]Grippetts (greh-PETS), facial, n. Any appendage or skinial formation suitable for the support of spoons. i.e. The nose is the major facial grippett whereas warts or acne would be considered minor grippetts.

THE SPOON HANG: HOW IT WORKS

fig b.

WHICH SPOON?

You would think all baseball bats are the same. Yet all players have their own special favorites. The same holds true for golfers and their putters. All this sports equipment looks the same to me, it all feels the same, but to the man that uses it and depends on it there must be a difference or why the big deal?

Spoon hangers experience the same problem when trying to select the best spoon.

When you first start you don't notice it, but the more you get into spoon hanging the more you'll begin to lean towards one specific spoon or ladle. On the following page you'll see outstanding spoons and the outstanding features that support them.

FOUR EXAMPLES OF FRONTAL FACIAL FLATWARE

Spoonal Analysis: Which spoon doesn't fit? This random sampling demonstrates the spoonal advantage of the Windsor (right) above all others. Whereas the wooden is fine for stirring, the plastic goes well on picnics and the ladle is OK for soups, their hangability ratio is extremely low. On the other hand, the Windsor is the one spoon that can do it all. When it comes to spoonhanging, **don't leave home without it!**

"It is an established fact that through spoon hanging, participants reap the reward of wonderful, well shaped noses."

YOUR OWN NOSE

These two drawings illustrate all too clearly what can happen if your nose takes a wrong turn down the probiscus path.

The nose on the left, through Aerobospoonersize, has achieved not only a high level of beauty but it is also extremely functional. (note the exquisite demitascular nasal outlets (Fig. A.) as opposed to the tunnulational expandoports (Fig. B).

Note how in Fig. A the nose occupies a small portion of the face while in Fig. B the face occupies a small portion of the nose. This is a typical example of mid-face spread, an all too common result of the unbodulated nose.

The well bodulated nose, conscientiously maintained through a realistic program of aerobospoonersize, spoon hanging and plenty of fresh air can extend the life of you and your friendly probiscus for many many years while the unbodulated nose stands out like a beacon in the night as a warning to all spoon hangers.

The well bodulated Aerobo spoonercised nose

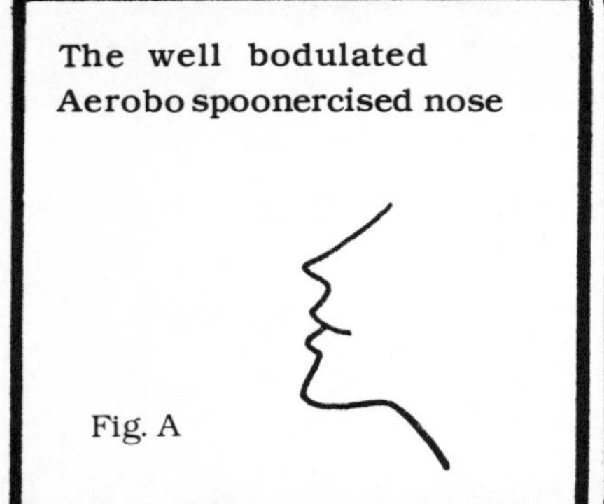

Fig. A

Mister Flabby Nose

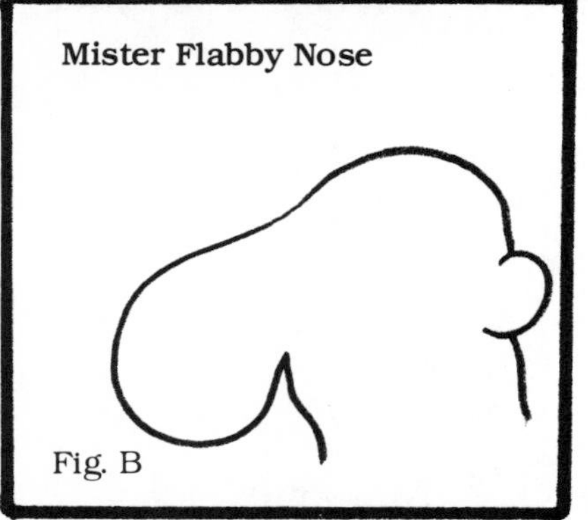

Fig. B

Benefits of Spoon Hanging: The Healthy Nose

It is an established fact that through spoon hanging, participants reap the reward of wonderful, well-shaped noses. It's easy to see why. Spoon hanging is the only form of exercise (bodulation) available to the probiscus.

> *"Goofy noses are made, not born."*
> *— Tony (Spoons) Lamott*

No one is born with a big nose. Did you ever see a baby with a big nose? Of course not. Bad noses are made not born. And here's something to make you think: It is a little known fact but big noses may be the single largest cause of highway fatalities. Here's why . . .

The road as seen through the eyes of a normal driver.

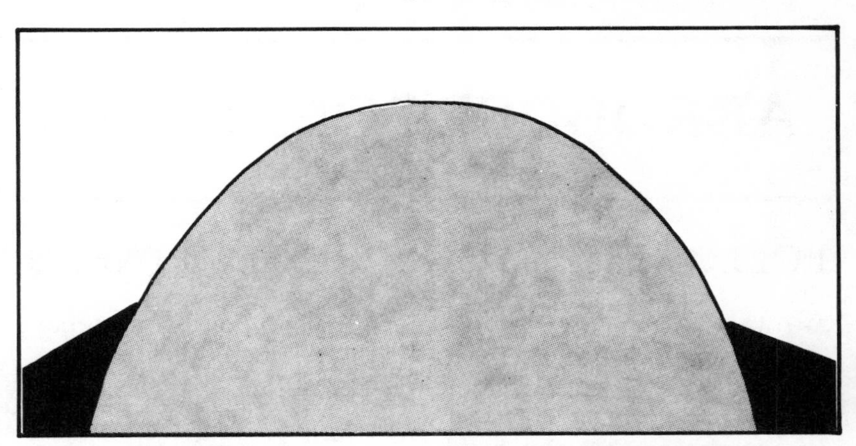

The same road as seen through the eyes of a BIG NOSED driver.

Shocking but true, and unfortunately nothing is being done about it. Saddest of all, from all appearances the people in charge, our own elected officials, may very well be the biggest offenders.

Fortunately as the popularity of spoon hanging increases nasal protuberances will diminish in direct proportion. So the future need not be as bleak for the unwary pedestrians, who have just as much right to the streets as their bulb-nosed killers.

The nose is your leader, follow it, take care of it. A healthy leader is a wise leader and through a careful program of nasal fitness and Aerobospoonercize not only will you achieve this goal but in the process reap many other benefits, among them lower insurance rates.

"Don't let a friend drive if he's got a big nose."

— Tony (Spoons) Lamott

Are You a Highway Hazard?

Here's a simple test to check your nasal health.

Cross your eyes. You chould be able to make out the tip of your nose. If you don't have to cross your eyes to do this I suggest you change your address immediately, paint your car and begin an intense program of AEROBOSPOONERCIZE at your earliest convenience.

AEROBOSPOONERCISE

FOLLOWING YOUR NOSE TO FITNESS

Aerobospoonercize is the logical common sense method for achieving top physical and mental condition. It is based on the theory that the body must follow the nose and it's this kind of practical reasoning that makes it the sound program it is.

Think about it. Where has your body gone that your nose hasn't already been? On the surface this sounds silly, stupid and naive . . . **and that's why it's been overlooked.**

Aerobospoonercize has been developed for the express purpose of carrying out nature's plan of order in attaining physical and mental well being. It is a program that, if followed to the letter, is geared to make you stronger, faster, brighter, and depending on your age, taller than you've ever been before.

Bubbles (Trixie) Laterno

YOUR AEROBOSPOONERCISE INSTRUCTOR

Bubbles (Trixie) Laterno loves "people, clear wine, and hiking in the mountains with my boyfriend." She grew up in Southern California, graduated from M.I.T., is an aspiring author, and an expert baton twirler. Aerobospoonercize is just one side of her "multitudinal personality". It allows her the freedom she needs to express her "inner creativity" and considers it one of her "contributions to the sexual revolution". When not hiking, bodulating or batoning she is busily working on her semi-autobiographical novel, **Twenty-five Great Parades.**

THE HEALTHY NOSE

Bodulation Number One

For the development of the frontal tipiscular area of the nose known as the Probisca-ball, Bodulation #1 is the perfect exercise.

Step #1

Hold two plebian spoons at eye level no more than 3 inches from face. Quickly begin breathing in and out with tongue extended in a panting

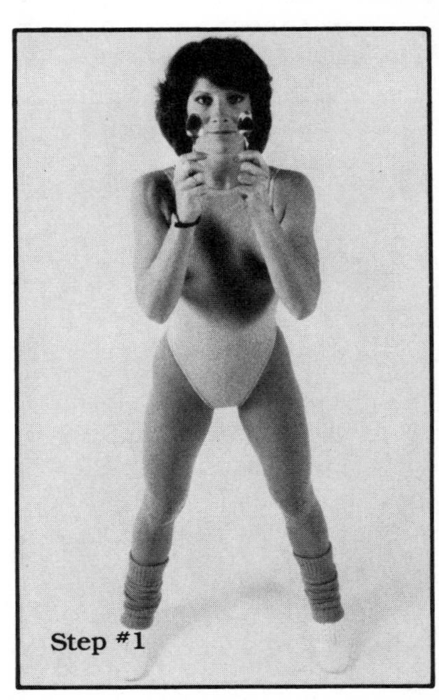

Step #1

motion until both spoons are fully fogged . . . this will give you all the privacy you need.

Step #2
Without bending your elbows stretch arms outward as shown in figure #2. The spoons at this point should be even with your shoulders. While keeping your head straight, look at the spoons. You should be able to see them out of the corners of your eyes. Pull the spoons back as far as you can, making sure to keep both of them in sight at all times.

This Bodulation will not only expand your peripheral vision but as you progress and are able to hold the spoons farther and farther back, it will also make you a great topic of conversation among your friends.

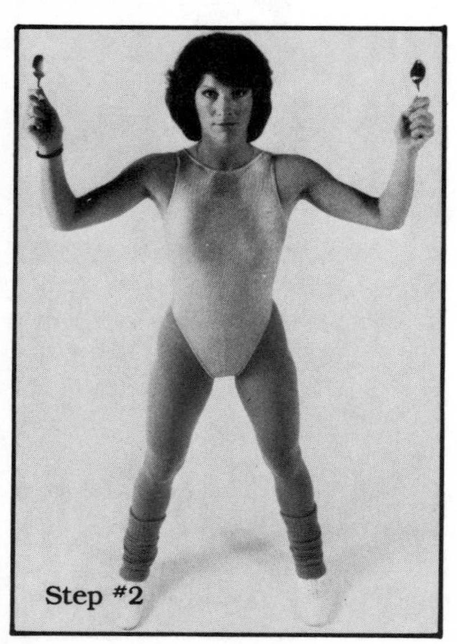
Step #2

Step #3

Step #3
Place the spoons on your cheeks as shown. This is done to prepare the nose for the spoonal placement in Step #4 and is a safeguard against post nasal shock.

Step #4
Place the spoons on your nose and please remember that the nose is the most important part of the body so great care is advised during this particular Bodulation. You have now reached the peak of this Bodulation . . . the three spoons forming a triad of power which is now focusing itself **all over the place!** This is known as **the good part** and the position should be held for as long as you have time.

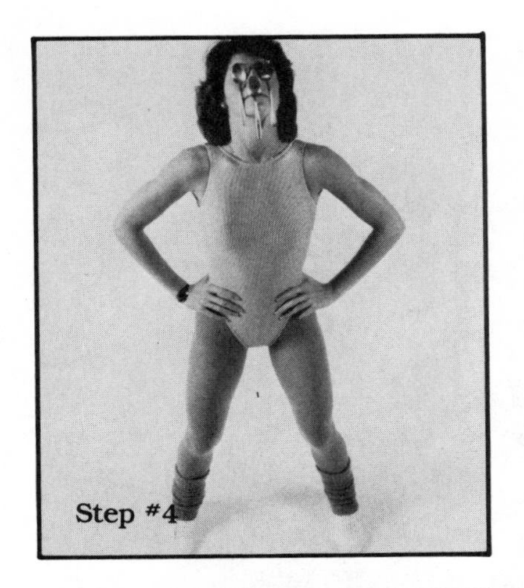
Step #4

Follow these rules to the letter and within weeks you'll see the beginnings of your new Aerobospoonercizical life. Pounds of unsightly flesh will disappear, inches, and in some cases maybe even feet, of unwanted nasal growth will vanish before your very eyes.

Keep it up. You are on your way to complete nasal fitness.

1. A Bodulation is a specific exercise in the overall Aerobospoonercize program. Bodulation #1 is by far the most popular of the 27 basic Bodulations.

CARE OF YOUR SPOONS

Now that you realize the importance of taking proper care of your nose, it is important to remember that equal attention should be paid to the rest of your gear . . . your spoons. The importance of maintaining your finely tuned state-of-the-art equipment cannot be taken lightly. Many a hanger has come to rue the day his championship spoon was left overnight in a bowl of slowly solidifying cereal. And how many times have they found themselves searching endlessly for their favorite spoon, only to have it turn up in the backyard sandbox or in that forgotten carton of ice cream in the basement freezer?

Remember, there are spoons and there are spoons. Naturally you will want your "gear" kept separately from the family eating utensils. Storage boxes are sold specifically for this purpose. That, along with a good silver polish and a good chamois are all you really need.

Where spoons are concerned cleanliness is the key. Always wash your spoons in plenty of hot water using a mild dishwashing liquid and a soft cloth. Rinse off, again in plenty of hot water and allow to air dry. Do **not** towel dry. And about once a month, depending upon frequency of play, get out that silver polish and chamois, find yourself a nice quiet spot, and spend the afternoon getting your gear in shape.

When instructing children in the fine art of spoon hanging spoonists learn the importance of taking care of their equipment. Here a wonderful father provides spoonal instruction with an instrument which was **not** towel dried.

"N.O.S.E. is not one of those things that means many things to many people. N.O.S.E. is the National Organization for Spoonhanging Enthusiasts."

6 YOUR N.O.S.E.

Tony (Spoons) Lamott. Current President of N.O.S.E.

N.O.S.E. THE ORIGINS

N.O.S.E. (The National Organization of Spoon Enthusiasts) is the governing body for all spoon hanging events. This chapter will explain its position in professional spoon hanging and its affect on you as a competitor.

N.O.S.E. takes a firm stand on many positions, though it is an organization subject to caprice and whim, and may waffle at any time freeing itself to take an entirely opposing view even unto itself. More than once the sport was forced to come to a dramatic halt while its governing body was deadlocked with itself and could not come to agreement over some fine point of the game.

Competitors in the sport of spoon hanging are required by the Rules Committee to be fully aware of all new regulations in its ever changing code book, and N.O.S.E. is proud to report that in the entire history of the sport, there has never been an infraction. It is with this same pride that N.O.S.E. operates entirely on the honor system. They strongly believe that to police the competitive spoon hanger and bring him down to the level of a common criminal would destroy the solid chain

N.O.S.E. NEW HANG CERTIFICATE

Awarded this 15 day of June, 19 84.

This is to certify that Wendy Mullroy has originated a new spoon hang which has been duly recorded in the N.O.S.E. archives.

Hang Name "Wendy Windsor"

Tony

Tony (Spoons) Lamott, President

New Hang certificate awarded to Wendy Mullroy 1/8/84

of faith and trust that has been built through years of loyalty, faith and dedication. (Though rules now under consideration may change this at any moment)

N.O.S.E. is not one of those things that means many things to many people. N.O.S.E. means the National Organization for Spoon Enthusiasts. It is a proud institution dedicated peripherally and indirectly to more things than the average man sees in a day. It is not just a name that is synonymous with taste and fine clothes everywhere . . . it IS spoon hanging.

Founded on the belief "If a man can hang a spoon he should be able to do it in such a way where we all can benefit" it has thrived and grown to this day where not one of its members can look back and say that those aren't spoken words of opinion.

N.O.S.E. operates for the good of spoon hangers everywhere. That includes YOU. So remember, it's your N.O.S.E. Support it.

SOME N.O.S.E. FUNCTIONS

N.O.S.E. is the governing body for all (EVERY) sanctioned spoon hanging competition. It sets all rules, collects all funds, distributes all awards and in the process answers to no one.

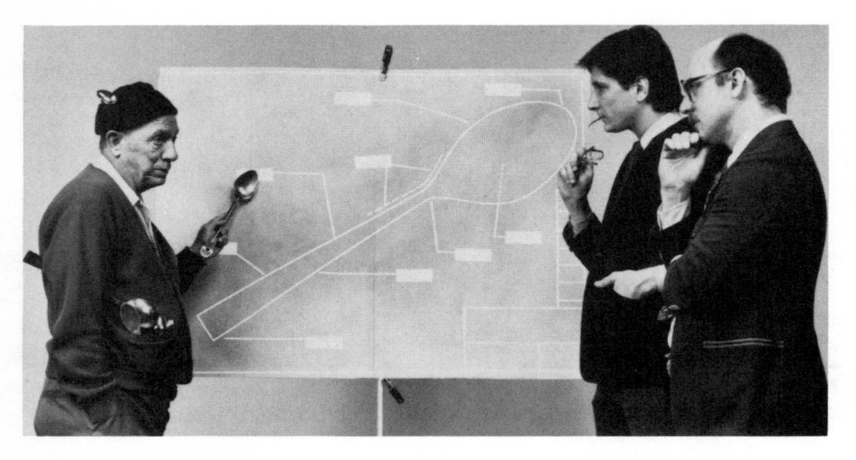

Helps set standards for spoon manufacturers. Spoon manufacturers, knowing the importance of keeping hangers happy, regularly seek the advice and guidance of the president of N.O.S.E.

Maintains N.O.S.E. archives. Records all new hangs, national and international records and keeps detailed files on all new spoon models developed.

Inducts honorees into "N.O.S.E. Legends in Their Times." A vote of 82% of the sportswriters from the top 400 international newspapers is all you need to qualify.

Records all new hangs and awards certificates to hangers. When photo and other proof of a new hang are submitted to N.O.S.E., official "New Hang" certificates are issued.

Issues site sanction certificates and awards to be given out at hang. Having a private hang? Want to pass out official 1st, 2nd or 3rd place certificates? Just contact N.O.S.E. They also collect fees. You think all of these awards and certificates are free?

PLAYSPOON INTERVIEW:

TONY (SPOONS) LAMOTT

A candid conversation with the current president of N.O.S.E. and the most legendary spoonist of all time.

The field of competitive sports is filled with great innovators: men and women who against all odds and with great personal sacrifice have fought to have their dreams become a reality. Tony (Spoons) Lamott is one of these people.

Tony (Spoons) Lamott didn't just create Spoon hanging. Tony (Spoons) Lamott **is** *spoon hanging. Fifty years ago in a sleepy little town called Spoon River, Illinois, Tony said his first word — "SPOON". For fifteen years he had remained silent. For fifteen years he was unsure, but on that day Tony (Spoons) Lamott made his decision and he let the world know. Spoon hanging was born. This frail boy, an outcast, a lonely troubled youth with little more than a kindergarten education and a knack for the triangle, had done something that would not soon be forgotten.*

Tony (Spoons) Lamott was born on April 19, 1920, the ony son of a bait shop and boat rental tycoon. He enjoyed the good life and the best of what Spoon River had to offer.

His father loved him dearly but was embarrased to show it, as was his mother, for fear of what the townspeople would think, but they were all very polite. The family business was located five miles from the river and depended heavily on the annual flood for its profit. To finance his dream of spoon hanging Tony opened a sandbag factory. It was an instant success. The river, banked on all sides by Lamott's bags, would never flood again. With the financial foundation for spoon hanging now secure, Tony (Spoons) Lamott set off on his campaign to enlighten the world about spoon hanging.

"Spoon hanging clearly explodes the myth that there is a reason for everything."

"I've never used my prowess as a spoon hanger to take advantage of the opposite sex . . . but that doesn't mean I've stopped trying."

It wasn't all peaches and cream yet. The sandbag factory had put the family bait shop and boat rental into bankruptcy. His father, despondent and a ruined man now, spent his days sitting in a small boat, oars in hand, staring across the fields waiting for the water to come; while his loyal wife, Tony's mother, would stand by in foul-weather gear screaming, "Help, I'm drowning," to cheer him up. Tony loved his parents dearly and promised he would someday make up for all their hardship by naming a spoon hang especially after them.

The deepest regret in Tony's life is that they passed away before he was able to achieve this goal. But I know Tony and I know by the look in his eye and the determination in his face that someday he will. I believe in Tony (Spoons) Lamott.

We felt it was time to send veteran Spoonboy interviewer Joe Martin for an extended chat with Lamott about his life and times and spoons. Martin reports:

In the three days that I spent in Tony's retreat above a cleaner's on Chicago's near-north side, the legendary hero of spoon hanging told me many things. From the historic moment when he defiantly hung that first spoon from the tip of his nose in protest over a sloppily prepared bowl of farina, to the present day and the International headquarters and Spoon hanger's Hall of Fame where he is held in high honor, Tony (Spoons) Lamott is truly a man of destiny.

Later in the week we continued our interview at N.O.S.E. National Headquarters where I watched Tony open the mail and play with his Rolladex.

PLAYSPOON: Tony (Spoons) Lamott, do you feel obligated to carry spoons with you all the time because of your middle name?

LAMOTT: To be honest with you, Joe, it's the other way around. I know this sounds crazy but I actually got that nickname because I always carried spoons.

PLAYSPOON: It is said that the people of Spoon River are extremely protective of their image and once had the name of a popular song and movie theme changed because of it.

LAMOTT: That's true. "Spoon River" . . . great tune. The movie was

"If something is whiter than white, what color is it?"

"I know this sounds crazy but I actually got my nickname because I always carried spoons."

"Breakfast at Tiffany's" so you can see the title "Spoon River" was a natural. It didn't make a whole lot of sense when they changed it but it was a last minute thing and I guess they figured the melody would carry it through.

PLAYSPOON: Is it true that they will not insure a film if it has a spoon hang sequence?

LAMOTT: Yes, unfortunately there were two bad experiences where the movie stars, because they failed to follow N.O.S.E. safety standards, hurt themselves, Since then no one wants to take a chance. The films were "Chinatown" with Jack Nicholson and "Cat Ballou" with Lee Marvin.

"Some day I'd like to walk into traffic court and see a sign hanging behind the judge that reads 'No Spoons Allowed'."

PLAYSPOON: What gave you the idea that competitive spoon hanging would make it?

LAMOTT: I was at the Super Bowl. I kept thinking Super Bowl . . . Super Bowl. And then it dawned on me that there was something missing . . . and the rest is history.

PLAYSPOON: A football player might compare himself to a rocket blasting through a human wall of steel. Skiers say skiing is like flying on a cloud. How would you describe spoon hanging?

LAMOTT: Imagine the spoon is a howling electric fan and the nose is a can of sardines with a giant hexagon walnut coming out of the top. Need I say more?

PLAYSPOON: No.

PLAYSPOON: Tony (Spoons) Lamott, after years of effort on your part, now that spoon hanging has finally become accepted, what would you say is the most personally rewarding aspect of it?

LAMOTT: All my life, no matter where I went, people would always tell me that there was a reason for everything that happened in this universe. Well, I believe that it is safe to say that spoon hanging clearly explodes this myth.

PLAYSPOON: What would you say is the major difference between competitive spoon hanging and any other competitive sport, let's say football?

LAMOTT: Spoon hanging is the only multi-practical sport in existence today. The spoon is functional as well as sportingly competitive. It can be used for eating, and it can be used as an aid to putting on your shoes and it is also a musical instrument. What else can you use a football for?

PLAYSPOON: Are there any dreams you still have for spoon hanging?

LAMOTT: Just one . . . Some day I would like to walk into traffic court and look up and see a sign hanging behind the judge that reads: "NO SPOONS ALLOWED."

When any two or more people are gathered in the name of spoon hanging it is inevitable that arguments and fisticuffs will break out over misinterpretation of the rules.

7 N.O.S.E. RULES & REGULATIONS

OFFICIAL N.O.S.E. RULES

Not to be confused with hanging "just for the fun of it", a N.O.S.E. sanctioned event is serious business. An official sanctioned event is a gathering of two or more people with the expressed intent of hanging spoons to qualify for awards certificates or to prove they have created a new hang they wish certified and placed in the N.O.S.E. archives.

When any two or more people are gathered in the name of spoon hanging it is inevitable that arguments and fisticuffs will break out over misinterpretation of the rules.

Although it is impossible to include all of the official N.O.S.E. rules for spoon hanging here, I have listed the most important. For a complete set of do's and don'ts, send $4.95 to N.O.S.E. for a copy of Tony Lamott's Book of Obscure Rules and Regulations for International Spoon Hanging Competition.

Section I. Legal Hangs

Sec. I Article A. Before a hang can be considered complete both hands must be below the waist (or at least 6 feet from the nasal passages) and the spoon must remain on the facial area of competition for no less than the count of ten. (see variations on competitive hangs.)

Sec. I Article B. No foreign matter may be used to implement the hanger in spoonal affixation. (i.e. glues, sticky matter, tapes, staples, tacks, etc.)

See Sec. I, Art. B.

Sec. I Article C. No competitor may touch, be touched, jostle or be jostled by any participants (spectatorial or otherwise) without causing the foulization of the event. (see foulization of event) or unless otherwise specified (see diversionary practices)

Sec. I Article D. Excessive head tilt is not allowed. What constitutes "excessive"? This is something you'll just have to work out.

Section II. Foulization of the Event

Foulization of the event can, and in many cases is, caused by any infraction of the N.O.S.E. code of rules and ethical practices. When this happens the event must start over with TEN points subtracted from the score of the perpetrator. More points of penulation (penalty points) may be dispensed at the judge's discretion depending on the seriousness of the offense and/or the mood of the judge himself.

Section III. Diversionary Tactics

Any direct or indirect action which compels the spoon to drop from facial zone of competitor. There are proper (approved) and improper (illegal) tactics. Although N.O.S.E. takes a firm stand as to which are proper it is generally agreed that all diversionary maneauvers be agreed upon at the outset of competition and are forbidden only in orthodox competition.

Sec. III Article A. Proper (approved) Diversionary Techniques

Sec. II Article A (§1). The Alarming Statement ("look behind you!") or the Creative Warning ("what's that crawling up your leg?") are two examples of the most basic diversionary techniques. They are used most often in One-on-One competitions where the participant's victory is dependent on who can keep the spoon on the facial competition zone the longest.

The Alarming Statement. Sec. III, Art. A (§).

Sec. III Article (§2). The Insulating Malicious Statement: "Hey, fat ass" and "Up Yours, ______________________________ " (insert slang term for national origin here) are very popular, although many spoon hangers find great success with other odd or biological combinations. Malicious reference to family history and background seem to be especially effective.

Sec. III Article A (§4). The Elaborate Scheme.

This diversion is for the imaginative spoon hanger with the strong desire to win. It can range from the simple phone call to the complex multi-car collision outside the door.

Sec. III Article B. Improper (illegal) Diversionary Tactics

It is against N.O.S.E. policy to openly discuss illegal diversionary techniques because we don't want to give you any ideas. Below is one such example just so you know what we're talking about.

Improper Divisionary Tactic (Sec. III, Art. B)

Section IV. The Point System

In all but the Fast Draw One-on-One, which is judged only by who can hang a spoon first and fastest, points are used to determine the winner in all N.O.S.E. sanctioned events.

Points are given for various reasons. We will be dealing here with only those that apply to spoon hanging competitions, they are as follows:

Sec. IV Article A. Basic points. The actual hanging of the spoon.

Spoon number one .... ten points
Spoon number two .... twenty points
Spoon number three .... thirty points

At this point you should be picking up a pattern.

The more spoons you hang the more points you get. A spoon hanger who successfully hangs ten spoons would receive a total of five hundred and fifty points. If you're having trouble figuring out how I've reached this conclusion you are in the right sport.

Sec. IV Article B. Degree of Difficulty Points.

These are achieved, as implied, by the number of barriers the spoon hanger must overcome to complete the hang.

The alert spoon hanger can gain valuable bonus points by simply paying attention to his daily life and making sure he has his spoon ready to take advantage of any opportunities fate might offer.

If you think about it, most of us have been in situations where it would be extremely difficult to hang a spoon. Shown here are several examples: There are first the intermediate (normally not life-threatening) and then the maximum . . . where most points are awarded posthumously.

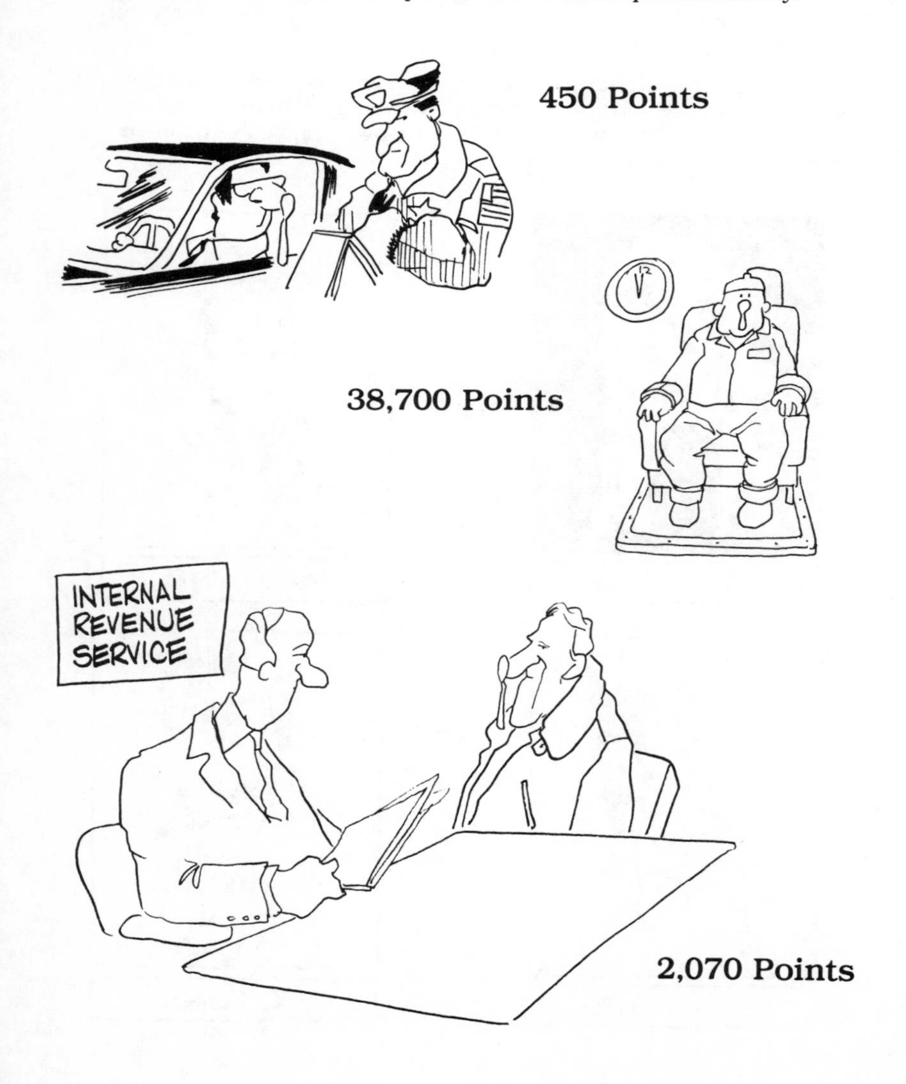

1,200 Points

800 Points

100 Points

Keep in mind that one of the benefits of situation spoon hangs is that proof is very simple. There is no need for photos or even an official N.O.S.E. judge, for in most cases the calamities that befall the spoon hanger usually become common knowledge within a short time and are even in many instances reported in the daily newspapers of the area.

N.O.S.E. has prestigious awards for any and all spoon hangers in this category. They need only be informed of the particulars (enclose newspaper articles or media information when possible).

Point range for situation hangs: 100-40,000 points.

Sec. IV Article C. Expression points.

Here are some examples of bonus points gained through facial contortions, expression or imitations.

Point allotment for expression can vary from 20 to 100 points and are determined at the judge's descretion on the basis or originality, foolishness and most importantly how much it effects the spoon itself.

fig 1) 80 points

Note how the spoons, originally in the standard double teardrop formation, are effected by the facial contortion (full toothed variation on a grin) that they are now in the much advanced VADARIAN FLYING SPOON WEDGE configuration, certainly one of the most challenging of all two spoon hangs.

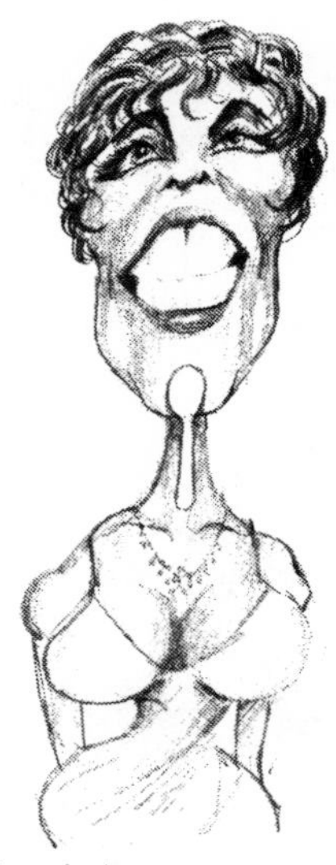

fig 2) 8 points

By comparison this spirited spoon hanger executing a perfect one spoon chin dangler (drool) is alloted only 8 expression points for the obvious reason that the spoon was left relatively uneffected. Unfortunately expression points are relegated to the area above the neck or this would certainly be a much different story.

Section V. Creating a New Hang

Have you created a new hang for our archives?

When Andy Warhol said that the day would come when everyone would be famous for 15 minutes he wasn't just blowing smoke. His words have become a reality for the imaginative spoon hangers shown below.

These inspired spoon hangers have made a place for themselves in the hallowed halls of N.O.S.E. If you have created a hang that you feel is of historical note and would like it made part of the permanent N.O.S.E. records, please send us a photo or description of the hang, and this handsome certificate emblazoned with the verification of your accomplishment will be sent the first chance we get.

Please enclose $4.95 to cover the cost of mailing, handling and pocket money for the staff. Also enclose name, address, date and time of hang, photograph, signature of witness and suggested name for hang.

Hang created 7/15/83
by Frank A Merble. Named
One Spoon Postal Pivot

Hang created 2/11/78
by Molly Watkins. Named
The Punkhang

Cheating: Why, When, Where and How

Cheating is a big part of every form of competitive sport. Many people look on it as a short cut to success. The spoon hanger is no different ethically and morally from anyone else. So, why not cheat?

Our researchers, after some digging, have come up with what we think are some legitimate reasons for playing fair. We are not so foolish or naive to believe these reasons are strong enough to offset the bountiful rewards the successful cheat might reap, but we do feel they offer a viable alternative. Here they are:

1) Winning without cheating is more satisfying. The competitor who wins honestly knows that he has earned his victory and may take a special pride in his achievement. (Note: This satisfaction is greatly diminished when the game is played for money. It takes a strong individual to pass up a guaranteed win, through the use of deceptive strategy, in favor of honor).

2) The ego trip. Winning without manipulative tricks, or clever diversions is like playing with one hand behind your back (for the experienced spoon hanger that is).

3) At this point the reasons for not cheating may begin to seem kind of shallow, and maudlin, golden rulish things, do unto others and so on, that everyone already knows. So rather than pulpitize you with our keen sanctimonious wit we are going to push on.

Cheating: The Viable Alternative. How To.

This heading may imply that we condone cheating. This couldn't be farther from the truth. My personal feeling is that I don't think it's a good idea and I really doubt that I could ever consider doing it in any form of spoon hanging competition, unless of course there was absolutely no other way to win, and even then I would seriously have to consider what would happen if I were to get caught.

But for those of you without ethics or a sense of moral obligation, please pay close attention. This is a very important section and could literally save your life. **Remember, N.O.S.E. does not condone cheating.**

Section VI. Basic Cheating (illegal techniques).

The following maneuvers are considered illegal and ill advised by the N.O.S.E. Rules Committee.

Sec. VI Article A. Excessive Head Tilt

This maneuver (covered earlier in definitive spoon hangs) is one of the most obvious yet simplest of hoaxes to pull off. Requiring only the use of the complete denial tactic it can prove to be a very formidable tool.

If your opponent complains that you were holding your head back, just deny it. Remember it is very important that you be firm on this point. Indignance is the key. Some people prefer the hurt look or even the "ok then, keep the damn money if you're gonna be that way" has been known to work quite well, especially when followed by a "that's the last time, pal, don't even talk to me . . ."

Develop your own style, and whenever possible compete with shorter, less physically developed hangers. It makes the collection less of a hassle.

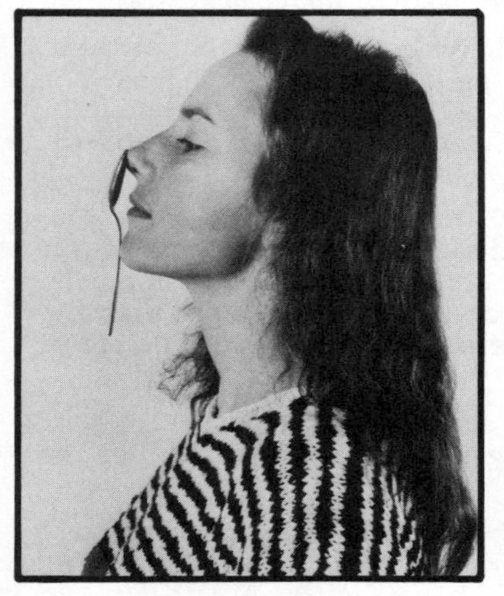

Brave

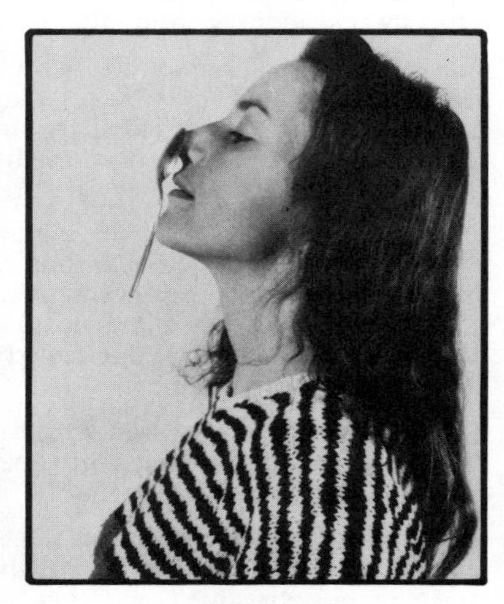

Braver

Bravest

Stupid

Sec. VI Article B. Rubber Cement. If you require any further explanations do not use this approach.

Sec. IV Article C. Paying off the judges.

(For an in-depth study on variations of this method and its universal appeal, look for my book "State and Federal Highways; Your Road to Financial Independence) soon to be available at fine bookstores everywhere.

Sec. VI Article D. Magnetic Implants. Historically one of the classic methods of cheating, the use of magnetic implants has become all but obsolete. They are considered far too cumbersome for present day use. (caution: magnetic implants should not be inserted in or around the eyeballs or eye sockets as they tend to attract all metal objects. More than a few overly zealous spoon hangers have found this out, with disastrous results at the dinner table.)

Artificial (Sticky) Skin. Section IV, Art. D.

The wonderful world of science has indeed achieved another grand success if the satisfied expression of this clever spoonist shown below is any indication.

Looks and feels like real skin

During competition

Drawback

To me, the artificial (sticky) skin seems to be the perfect answer. The spoon hanger's dream.

If there are any drawbacks it may be the occasional nuisance of flies, insects and lint which all seem to adhere more than one might hope.

"Remember that really stupid game called Charades? Well this is even better . . . group spoon hanging!"

PARTY GAMES

This chapter is devoted to the social aspects of spoon hanging: one-on-one competition, party hangs and the advantages of spoon hanging in the ever popular single's scene. You'll learn about Criss-Cross, the more genteel Add-a-Spoon and the sophisticated Pendulum Swing. Whatever your idea of fun, from the action packed Battling Spoons to wide opened public hangs, the sport of spoon hanging truly meets a need heretofore unfulfilled.

Would the World Boxing Association sponsor a fight in your living room? Would the N.B.A. sponsor a basketball tournament in your driveway? Would the U.S. Tennis Association let you hold a match in your back yard?

Highly doubtful.

But N.O.S.E., the International governing body of all spoon hanging events WILL. That's right, the National Organization of Spoon Enthusiasts, N.O.S.E. itself, will let you hold a fully sanctioned spoon-hanging meet, official awards and all, right in your very home. Provided you meet certain qualifications.

The opportunity to hold your own spoon-hang meets is your right. Take advantage of it. Throw out that Scrabble board. Jot a nice thank-you note and mail it to Parker Brothers along with your old Monopoly set and put that Trivia stuff right in the micro wave, or barbeque it. Remember that really stupid game called charades? Well, this is even better — group spoon hanging.

Would you believe there is an award sanctioned by N.O.S.E. (ITSELF) for the most spoons hung in a public eating house? Would you believe there's an equally prestigious award for pubs, ale houses, taverns, bars, taps, beer halls and old people's homes that are able to accomplish the same feat?

Well, it's all true, except for the old peoples' homes . . . there's no award for them. When they drop the spoons they won't pick them up and it turns into a big hassle with the nurses, and well, it's kind of a bad scene.

You're in a crowded subway and you are able to get everyone in it to hang a spoon on their nose? Depending on how you did it you may be eligible for a groupspoon hanging award, or some time in a state detention facility. Again, a lot hinges on how you did it.

"Once in my youth, I found myself in the awkward position of standing totally naked in a bedroom closet, while inches away, on the other side of the door, the love of my life barred the way while having a heated discussion with her husband.

I remember thinking, 'If only . . . If only I had a spoon to hang on my nose'."

— Tony (Spoons) Lamott

BATTLING SPOONS

This is a great action game where size is no barrier. Almost as much fun to watch as to participate in, Battling Spoons offers the ultimate challenge to aggressive players.

To begin, mark off floor space that is approximately 5 feet by 5 feet square. This will be the battling zone. Next, two opponents face each other outside the battle zone and hang a spoon. Both individuals then enter this zone with the purpose of dislodging their opponent's spoon, but **without touching said spoon.** Individuals may push, jar, tickle, or

Author and son Jay engaged in heated match of Battling Spoons

in any physical way cause their opponent's spoon to fall. Victory goes to the spoonist who can keep his spoon hanging the longest while remaining inbounds.

As you can probably tell, Battling Spoons is a great game for father-son competitions. Kids, because of their size and agility, do well against their bigger, yet bulkier and slower dads.

N.O.S.E. Rules:

1. The competitive zone must be clearly marked.
2. Never touch your opponent's spoon.
3. Remember to stay inbounds.
4. One point for each clear victory, ten points is considered "game".

ADD-A-SPOON

This is a nice quiet game for after dinner when everyone is sitting around the table. They're sipping coffee (good for warming spoons) and the subject of spoon hanging comes up, as it inevitably will.

Before the actual game begins, give everyone a chance to show off their favorite hangs. This serves to get everyone loosened up while warming up the spoons as well.

The host or hostess begins play by performing a One Spoon Monte and then passes the spoon counterclockwise around the table as each guest in turn performs the same hang (using the same spoon keeps it warm and provides all kinds of ammo for "nose grease" jokes.

When the spoon returns to the host he must then perform any two spoon hang and again pass the spoon to the next guest.

This continues, with those guests who cannot add-a-spoon dropping out (to great ridicule, of course). Note: if any guest is unable to continue adding a spoon, he or she may wish to lose their turn and stay in the game by consuming an alcoholic beverage of their choice as penalty.

N.O.S.E. Rules:

1. Add only one spoon at a time.
2. A time limit of no more than 2 minutes per hand should be established.
3. Use of diversionary tactics must be agreed upon before play begins.
4. If host is forced to drop out, player on his left becomes "spoon leader".

THE PENDULUM SWING

(A "betcha can't game")

The Pendulum Swing is the most challenging, yet personally satisfying of all hangs. While hanging a spoon the competitor attempts to swing it in a half circle. Sound impossible? This innovative hang is tricky and difficult but **can** be done.

Seat yourself in an armless chair at a table. Begin by hanging your spoon a little higher than usual on your nose. While facing forward, bend from your waist to the right side, allowing the spoon to swing with you. Bend until the bowl of the spoon is even with the table top.

Next, come back to the original upright position then repeat the bend to the left side. Congratulations? You've completed the Pendulum Swing.

Helpful hints:
Breathe out of the side of your mouth (in this hang too much spoonular condensation can cause excess slippage).

When passing center, at halfway point, tuck lips in close making sure to provide a comfortable area of Dangloinal Province between the spoon and mug (face).

Start

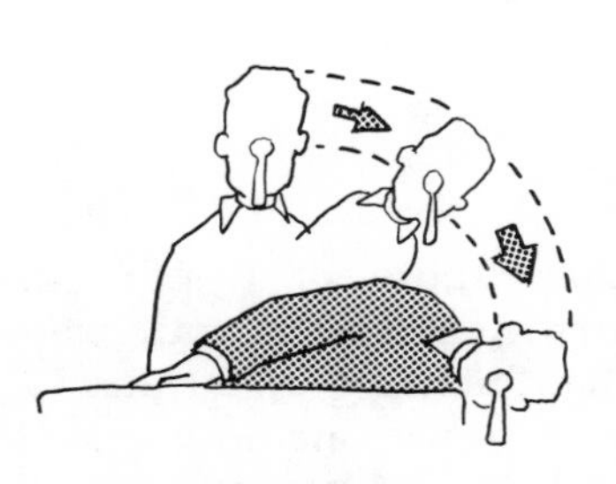

Half swing

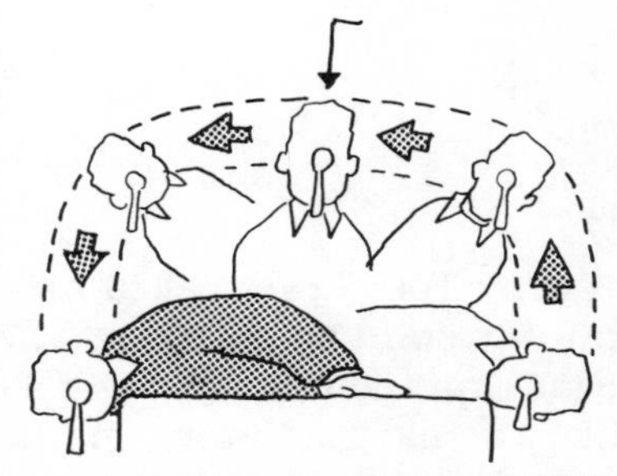

Full swing (completed)

THE FAST DRAW

"Like two gladiators battling in an arena, metal against metal, only one will walk away — the victor . . ."

— Tony (Spoons) Lamott

"Corny Tony" they called him, but his point is well made. The Fast Draw competition is a lot like the old gladiators, maybe more like the old West as speed plays more of a part than anything else as you'll see in the following diagrams. The trick to the one-on-one is skill and speed. A person with a cool hand and a hot spoon can make a fist full of money at this. There is probably no surer way of gambling than to bet on your own skills and this format puts all the cards in your hand. You can't blame the field goal kicker.

These two are obviously in a close match but there are no ties in spoon hanging. Eventually through some sneaky maneauver one opponent will get the other to drop his spoon without losing theirs. Ingenuity is the key.

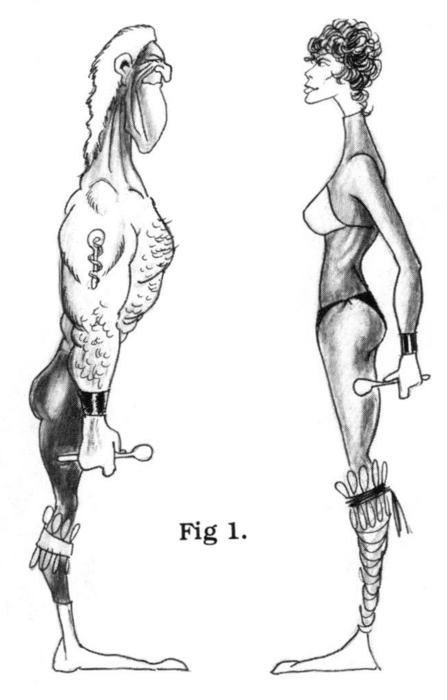

Fig 1.

Fig 1. Here we see the spoons in mid-point action on their way to the target . . . nose. This is comparable to watching the bullets in a gunfight. This is part of what makes spoon hanging such an interesting spectator sport as well. The other part is side betting, taken from a popular casino game, sometimes played against a wall in an alley.

Fig 2.

Fig 2. Here we see two clearly defined styles. The spoon hanger on the left seems to favor the popular, tight fisted ram squeeze, a method easily identified by the taut rigid muscle shifts in tandem with the gritting motion of the teethal area, a combination hard to beat.

The other approach, used deftly by the opponent on the right is the complex and alluring self-hypnotic double-eye gleam single digit with a finger spasm. Trancelike in many ways, this is a style reserved for the select few who eat only organic foods at health stores.

Fig 4. This is the part that counts. Any fool can get a spoon up to his nose. What we're here for is to see if he can make it stay there, and for how long. The only rule as far as interfering with another player is you are not allowed at any time to touch, or push, or in any way physically cause your opponent to drop their spoon. Although I guess you could if you wanted to. The rule of thumb in spoon hanging is you can usually do something IF YOU REALLY FEEL LIKE IT.

Fig 3. Here we see that both spoons have taken hold at the same moment. This happens from time to time and it is in these cases that the ingenuity of the spoon hanger comes into play.

This contest will be judged by who's left standing with a spoon on his nose, a much easier task than trying to figure out who got theirs up first. The rules fluctuate as does the whimsical nature of the sport, but in most competitions people get tired of watching after three minutes of nothing happening. At the three minute mark my suggestion is to allow pushing, or shoving, or start over.

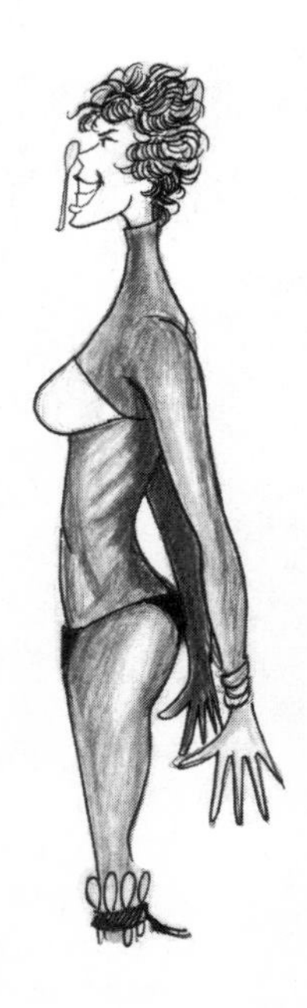

N.O.S.E. Rules

1. No opponent will introduce any foreign matter to help his spoon to hang.

2. No touching, pushing, tickling, or any physical contact is allowed between opponents.

3. Spoons must be at or below belt level when competition begins.

4. First person to hang a spoon wins. In case of an impactual tie, the person keeping his or her spoon hanging longest is the winner.

PASSING SPOONS

Now here's an intimate little game that's great for meeting people . . . where the worst players can sometimes have the most fun!

The basic idea is to get the spoon from the other player's forehead onto your nose without getting slapped. The photographs show the basic me-

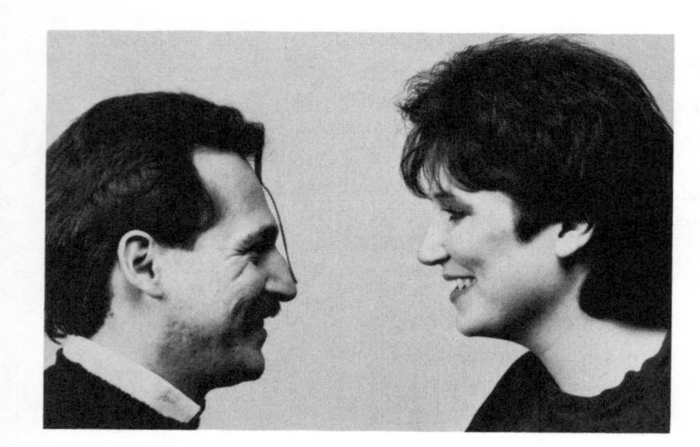

Fig 1.

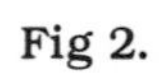

Fig 2.

Fig 3.

chanics of this novel stunt which, with a little practice, can be easily mastered.

There is however, one psychological problem. For some reason the close proximity of the players tends to touch off the tendency or urge in some people towards what we call "the lusty innovation". So before game time take care to check out your fellow players. You won't regret it. Remember: when playing Passing Spoons, "It's not **how** you play, it's **who**".

Fig 1. Here we see the spoonist on the right moving in for the nosal grab.

Fig 2. Here we see contact being made. The Probiscical (nosal tip) is now centrally implanted into the spoonal bowl.

Allow time for the fusion process to commence. Once the cohesion has taken place and you feel confident that the spoon is securely adhering to the nose, you may slowly begin to move your head backwards.

Fig 3. Here we see that calamitization has been avoided and the spoon passing is complete.

If there are more than two players the spoonist receiving the spoon must turn to the player on his or her left and implant the spoon somewhere on the headular domostructure (forehead) of that player. The One Spoon Central, or Goatal Horn hang is the recommended follow up hang.

"Everyone has someplace that they can hang a spoon better than anyone else sometimes."
— Tony (Spoons) Lamott

CRISS CROSS

Let's party!!

Few things excite the party going spoon hanger more than a wild game of Criss-Cross. The very nature of the game brings out that untamed bizarre abandonment spoon hangers so often refer to as their "meeting and greeting time".

Criss-Cross is not a game for the novice. To play effectively one must be able to hang at least three spoons while walking.

Here's how to play. Two teams and their spoons (usually 3 each) are set up at tables kitty-

corner from each other. To begin play one player from each team must successfully criss-cross the room with one spoon hanging, then with two spoons hanging, and so on. In turn, each team member must perform the same tasks. The first team to complete the tasks successfully wins.

N.O.S.E. Rules

1. Play begins when the first players on each team pick up their spoons.

2. In crossing the room, players should avoid any physical contact with each other.

BLIND MAN'S CRISS-CROSS (sans orbs)

When I said few things excite the party going spoon hanger more than a game of Criss-Cross, this was one of those things. This lively variation of Criss-Cross offers more surprises than some people care to deal with.

The object is for each player to reach the opposite side of the playing area. The first team to complete this wins. The second player may not begin to cross with his or her spoon until the first member of their team has completed the journey.

This game can be played with directions shouted from teammates to help avoid collisions (as in Deaf, Dumb and Blind Man's Criss-Cross.) Either way, it's sure to get someone a slap in the face if they know what they're doing.

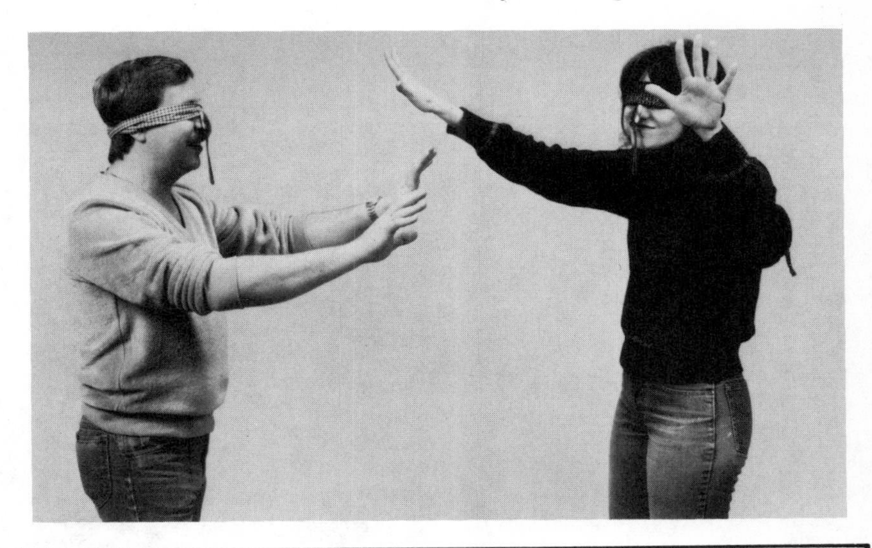

N.O.S.E. Rules:

1. Play begins as soon as either player, with blindfold in place, has hung his spoon.
2. Directions may or may not be shouted.
3. If directions are given, they need not be accurate. Use your imagination.
4. As in most spoon hang games or competitions, spoonists play **at their own risk!**

THE SINGLE'S SCENE

Up to this point we've described games and competitions. Entertaining diversions but certainly not very useful. Now let's look at a really important and socially significant side of spoon hanging . . . the pursuit of the opposite sex.

There's a certain something that a well-placed spoon adds to a guy that makes him different from the rest, sets him apart from the crowd, makes women sit up and take notice (in fact, it drives them wild!).

"First you gotta get their attention".

— Tony (Spoons) Lamott

Tony's got a point and there's nothing better to get the attention of the opposite sex than a face full of spoons. Try it yourself and see if you don't get immediate results.

You're tired of trying "Do you come here often?" and "What's your sign?". You're lonely and depressed. Nothing seems to work . . .

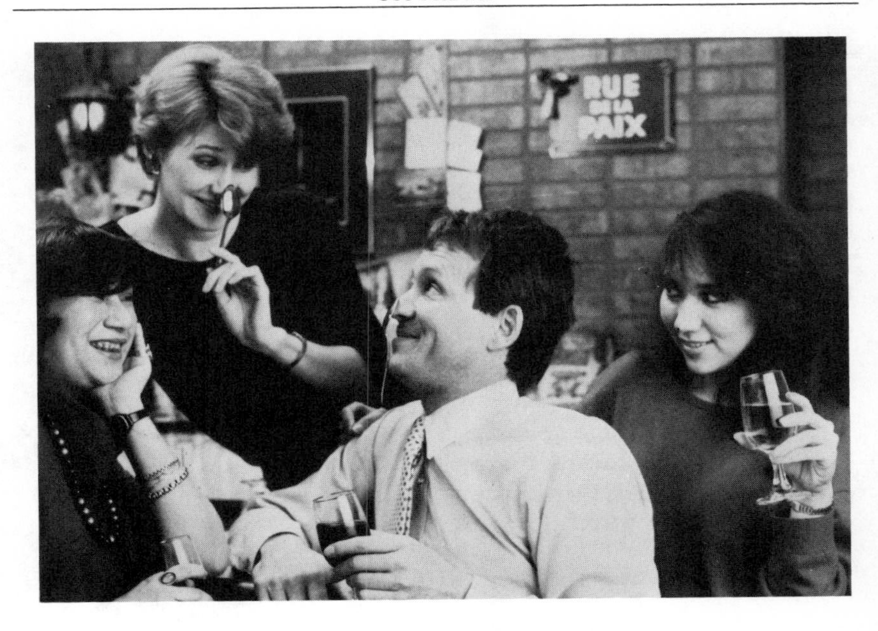

It really works! The well placed spoon drives them wild.

For the aggressive spoon hanger who wants more sure-fire results than provided by the One Spoon Monte, this fine example of the Quadra Spoon should do the trick.

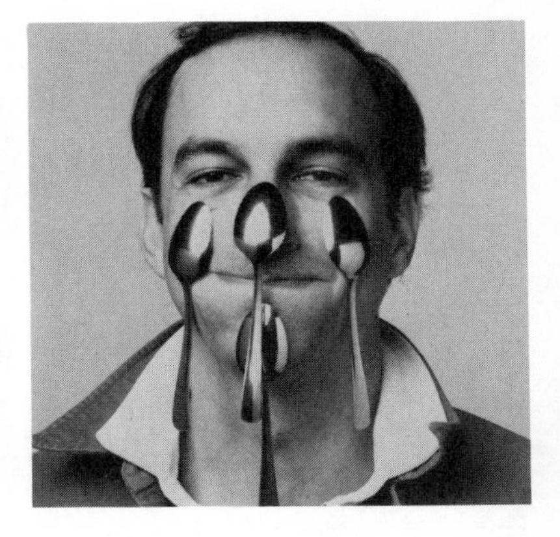

Here's a real attention grabber that's also great for hiding facial flaws like over ripe, fruit shaped noses and receding wimp chins: The Lower Facial Blot.

Bent Spoon Return

Danger Signal

If even spoon hanging can't help you or if simply more practice is in order, this is one of the signals to watch for.

YOUR VERY OWN WINDSOR MODEL HANGING SPOON

Every serious spoon hanger should own his or her very own Windsor model spoon. There are two very simple ways to accomplish this:

1. Simply send $1.25 to cover shipping and handling to: Spoons, c/o Turnbull & Willoughby, 1151 W. Webster, Chicago 60614 and we will send you your spoon FREE of charge.

2. Go to virtually any store in the known universe and you can purchase the common Windsor model or any other cheap spoon that will work just as well for about 25¢.